INTIMATE
DIRECT DEMOCRACY

"Modibo Kadalie's *Intimate Direct Democracy: Fort Mose, the Great Dismal Swamp, and the Human Quest for Freedom* is a powerful and accessible history of communities of resistance created and defended by Indigenous peoples and "self-emancipated" Africans in coastal regions of the southeastern United States. The untold underside of the history of colonial conquest, it is a narrative of those who did not destroy the earth with their "civilization" and their quest for profit but, rather, understood that their freedom depended on living in balance with each other, as part of the natural world. Vital reading for anyone interested in the history of the Southeast, *Intimate Direct Democracy* is a testament to the possibility of creating rich networks of sustainable, truly democratic alliances, and an inspiration to all who envision a liberated future."

—Natsu Saito, author of *Settler Colonialism, Race, and the Law: Why Structural Racism Persists.*

"Modibo Kadalie continues to give history new life and new perspective by raising questions about ecological crises both past and present. Direct democracy's answers to these inquiries, he tells us, are in its intimate relations. And the radical prospects for these connections are as clear as the intent in this new addition to his life's work."

—William C. Anderson, author of *The Nation on No Map* and co-founder of *Offshoot Journal.*

"Modibo Kadalie provides an innovative and original exposition of two eighteenth-century sites 'of defiance, resistance, freedom, and ecologically symbiotic intimacy': Fort Mose and the Great Dismal Swamp. Dr. Kadalie's personable political style invites the reader into the revealing history of these two colonial-era communities where Indigenous, African, and poor white people created social and ecological systems of survival independent of the profit-motivated European colonists. *Intimate Direct Democracy: Fort Mose, The Great Dismal Swamp, and the Human Quest for Freedom* gives voice to truths of American history that are not found in traditional texts.

—Yakini Kemp, Professor and former Chair of English and Modern Languages, Florida A&M University.

"Acclaimed scholar, political scientist, and Pan-Africanist, Modibo Kadalie's *Intimate Direct Democracy: Fort Mose the Great Dismal Swamp and the Human Quest for Freedom* explores a neglected aspect of Black Freedom fighters in North American in eighteenth century. This book is an eye-opening account for anyone who is seeking to learn from the past to understand the present. It provides valuable information to university students majoring in African history, African American studies, politics and international affairs. Moreover, it brings to light African-Islamic influences on the Iberian Peninsula in areas of architecture, seafaring and military technology. It is evident that the original name of the site was Fort Musa, an African Islamic name. The structure of the fort is also a replica of Moorish forts in Northwest Africa i.e. Ribat, al-Murabitun, meaning a fortress or place of retreat."

—Mohamed Haji Mukhtar, Professor of African and Middle Eastern History, Savannah State University. Author of *The Rise and Expansion of Islam in the Middle East.*

"Modibo Kadalie does something remarkable in this book, especially when set against the present-day turn toward authoritarianism and hopelessness: he gifts us a sense of promise, of what was and can be self-organized by peoples with 'freedom-seeking aspirations.' In Intimate Direct Democracy, using an equally intimate storytelling style, he invites us into the world of two maroon communities: the Great Dismal Swamp and Fort Mose. He humbly lets the histories of those who sought refuge from colonizers, enslavers, and nation-states speak for themselves. Yet Kadalie also brings these self-governing, multiracial, autonomous eco-communities to life, compellingly reminding us that social ecological communal lifeways and solidarity are indeed possible, even under the worst of conditions. An inspiring must-read, when we most need it!"

—Cindy Milstein, Editor of *Deciding for Ourselves: The Promise of Direct Democracy.*

INTIMATE
DIRECT DEMOCRACY

FORT MOSE, THE GREAT DISMAL SWAMP, AND THE HUMAN QUEST FOR FREEDOM

Modibo Kadalie

Edited and Introduced by Andrew Zonneveld

On Our Own Authority! Publishing
Atlanta, Georgia

Intimate Direct Democracy: Fort Mose, The Great Dismal Swamp, and the Human Quest for Freedom
By Modibo M. Kadalie
Edited and introduced by Andrew Zonneveld

© 2022 On Our Own Authority! Publishing

Published collaboratively with the Autonomous Research Institute for Direct Democracy and Social Ecology in Midway, Georgia.

ISBN: 979-8-9856682-0-9
LCCN: 2022901943

On Our Own Authority! Publishing
Atlanta, Georgia.

www.oooabooks.org
oooabooks@gmail.com

Cover art by Megan Leach

To the freedom seekers of the past as we continue the quest today and into the future together.

CONTENTS

FIGURES

MODIBO KADALIE'S CRITICAL HISTORIOGRAPHY OF NORTH AMERICAN MAROONAGE

An introduction by Andrew Zonneveld

I first visited the Fort Mose Historic State Park with Dr. Modibo Kadalie in January 2016. At the time, I was almost completely unfamiliar with the history of Fort Mose and couldn't have guessed at the remarkable history of Black autonomy that had unfolded just outside of St. Augustine, Florida in the early eighteenth century. I also had not guessed at the personal importance of this site to Modibo. For as long as I've known him, Dr. Kadalie has always shared his concerns over public history. It's not unusual for him to call me when I'm traveling and recommend a particular museum, state park, or other public history site that he has already visited. "Go there. Look around. Then call me and let me know what you think," is his usual advice. When we visited the Fort Mose park and museum in 2016, however, I could tell that this site was especially significant to him. On the wall to the right of the museum entrance, I noticed his name engraved on a plaque that lists "Lifetime Members" of the Fort Mose Historical Society. As we toured the facility, Dr. Kadalie shared his evaluation of the museum's presentation of history—both its insights and oversights—and his sense of pride in what St. Augustine's Black community had accomplished in their commemoration of this site. This was also the day when he first shared with me his plans to write a book on Fort Mose.

Since that time, the project has evolved into a comparative study of Fort Mose with another site of radical Black autonomy on the Atlantic coast, the Great Dismal Swamp, which straddles the border of what is now Virginia and North Carolina. Dr. Kadalie's work on this manuscript

Figure 1. Entrance to Fort Mose Historic State Park.
Photograph by Andrew Zonneveld, July 2021.

continued throughout the course of our compiling his 2019 book, *Pan-African Social Ecology: Speeches, Conversations, and Essays* and throughout the world-shattering events of the 2020–2021 coronavirus pandemic and the directly democratic social uprisings that erupted across the United States following the racist police murder of George Floyd in Minneapolis in the summer of 2020. As the manuscript developed, the scope of Dr. Kadalie's writing expanded into a wide-angle view of social history, contextualizing the emergence of maroon communities in southeastern North America.

In studies of anti-colonialism and Black freedom movements, there are few subjects more powerful or more evocative than the maroons: individuals, families, and communities who emancipated themselves from slavery, escaping bondage to create their own communities of resistance on the peripheries of the empires that had once kidnapped, trafficked, enslaved, and policed them. Avid readers of history may be familiar with the maroons of Jamaica or Guyana, or even the Garifuna of Honduras, but maroon communities of the North American continent are often overlooked. It is also often forgotten that the first underground railroad did not travel north, but south to Spanish Florida.

Black autonomy, though, has always been a focus of Dr. Kadalie's life and work. He grew up in Riceboro, a rural Gullah-Geechee community on the Georgia coast. In past interviews, Modibo has recalled that his early life in the Georgia lowcountry was characterized by a "rich African influence."[1] Geechee people today are the direct descendants of Africans who were enslaved by profiteering white settlers to cultivate rice, sugar, and cotton for sale on an international market. The Gullah-Geechee people have managed to retain a remarkable multitude of traditional African cultural expressions in their language, dance, and worship, among other practices. Their communities have roots in maroonage and proliferated in the years following the United States Civil War, during which time they seized and redistributed former plantation lands among themselves. Many Geechee families still live on these lands, which they have held since the Reconstruction era.

Over more than six decades of activism—from the 1960 Atlanta lunch counter sit-ins to the League of Revolutionary Black Workers and the African Liberation Support Committee in the 1970s, to his participation in labor strikes and community self-defense movements in the 1980s, to his founding of the Autonomous Research Institute for Direct Democracy and Social Ecology in 2017—Dr. Kadalie has remained committed to the idea that the most oppressed peoples on earth can and do create revolutionary social change on a global scale through self-organization and direct action in their own communities, a perspective rooted in his Geechee coast upbringing.[2] Social intimacy is another crucial component of Dr. Kadalie's worldview. For him, closeness with one's peers and neighbors is the foundation of autonomy and self-governance because it provides groups of individuals with an opportunity to associate without hierarchy. Intimate connections such as these have always lent themselves to collective decision making and intra- and inter-communal solidarity.

---

1   Modibo Kadalie, interviewed by Matthew Quest, 12 November 2010, Voices of Labor Oral History Project, Southern Labor Archives. Special Collections and Archives, Georgia State University.

2   Dr. Kadalie's lifetime of activism is more comprehensively explored in his previous book, *Pan-African Social Ecology: Speeches, Conversations, and Essays* (Atlanta: On Our Own Authority!, 2019).

In his study of Fort Mose and the Great Dismal Swamp, he pulls on the historical thread of "intimate direct democracy" that weaves together seemingly disparate events—not only in eighteenth-century North America, but throughout many points in human history. For Kadalie, humans have an almost innate desire for social intimacy and autonomy. Even in the face of horrific oppression, ordinary people throughout history collectively strive for more fulfilling lifestyles in which they can live cooperatively with one another and, importantly, with the rest of the natural world. Using these principles as a guiding framework, Kadalie examines the interrelation of social and ecological crises throughout the long (and continuing) period of genocidal colonialist violence in North America, using these two maroon communities as focal points.

Kadalies's writing also demonstrates the inseparable relationship between the African maroons of the Great Dismal Swamp and Fort Mose and North America's Indigenous peoples, especially in the southeastern region of the continent, where maroon and Native communities occupied many of the same spaces as they resisted or evaded the violence of European colonialism. Histories of the Powhatan, Tuscarora, Yamasee, Muscogee, and Seminoles, among others, are considered in this work. The latter represents a special case. The Seminoles, Kadalie explains, are a multi-racial and multi-ethnic society that emerged in conscious resistance to European expansion and was labeled as "Indian" by the state in order to justify U.S. military campaigns of aggression and forced removal.

Part One of the book focuses on the social and ecological history of the Great Dismal Swamp, beginning with its natural history and earliest Indigenous inhabitants. Kadalie presents the era of European colonialism as a disastrous "clash of ecological perspectives," especially with regard to the swamp. While vast swamplands were seen as "dismal" and foreboding to the eye of European colonizers, these same spaces were sites of natural abundance for Indigenous peoples and soon became zones of autonomy for self-emancipated African maroon communities. Moreover, Kadalie argues that those communities inhabiting the Great Dismal Swamp throughout history—Indigenous, African, and other multi-racial societies—have shown "no sign" of social hierarchy in their archeological record. He extrapolates that these eco-communities were likely governed through a socially intimate form of direct democracy, in which individuals worked cooperatively for their collective benefit and did so without harming the swamp ecology. Individuals and families moved into the swamps not only to escape the brutality of slavery and colonialism, but also to recapture the freedom to govern their own lives in democratic harmony with one another and in symbiosis with their ecological surroundings.

Kadalie also clarifies that the swamp itself, as much as the people inhabiting it, represented a resistance to colonialism and emerging capitalism due to its unsuitability for large-scale agricultural exploitation. Kadalie then charts the proliferation of enslaved-labor farming during English colonialism in the region, a social, economic, and agricultural regime that is commonly been referred to as "the plantation system" by mainstream historians. In the present work, however, Kadalie breaks with that language so as to be more specific with regards to the racist violence endemic to capitalist agriculture in the colonial Americas.

Part Two shifts focus southward to Spanish-occupied Florida, charting the history of Gracia Real de Santa Teresa de Mose, or Fort Mose, which is widely considered to be the first free African town in North America. African families and individuals escaping slavery in the English colonies arrived here seeking freedom and autonomy behind Spanish colonial lines. They built their own town less than two miles north of the Spanish city of St. Augustine. In this remarkable place, they lived and worked as members of the greater St. Augustine settlement. They formed a militia and fought against their former English enslavers to defend Spanish territory and then successfully petitioned the Spanish Crown to formally recognize their freedom. While some historians describe Fort Mose as primarily an endeavor of Spanish colonial policy, Kadalie argues that the reality of its origin was quite the opposite. Spanish policy was, in fact, merely responding to the self-directed mobilization of African peoples in their autonomous quest for freedom. As Kadalie has stated elsewhere:

> [T]he policy of a government is epiphenomenal, meaning it is always a response to something. When I say epiphenomenal, I mean something that appears to be real but is not real in the form that it appears. For instance, moonlight does not come from the moon, but it's the

sunlight reflected by the moon. So too are these policies really reflections of social movement. Policies do not initiate anything. The government sees some kind of need, which it defines based on its own interests, and then institutes whatever program, whatever policy— war policy or welfare policy—it needs to stay afloat.[3]

The Spanish Crown's sponsorship of Fort Mose is a perfect example of this phenomenon. The Crown recognized that Africans were fleeing south from the English colonies on their own authority and saw in this an opportunity to use the situation to bolster their defenses against British military incursions while simultaneously undermining the expanding slave-labor farm economy in the Carolina colony. The actual movement of self-emancipated African people south into Spanish Florida, however, predated the Spanish policy.

The Fort Mose settlement was built, inhabited, evacuated, and destroyed twice over in the years from 1738 to 1812. Its first incarnation, founded in 1738, lasted only two years. Dr. Kadalie considers this period in particular to have been a genuine example of intimate direct democracy: a town that was conceived, planned, and built by a group of people who had emancipated themselves from enslavement—a manifestation of their desire and capacity for self-governance.

In 1740, General James Edward Oglethorpe of England invaded Florida and briefly captured Fort Mose. The African militia fought back and drove the English out during what became known as the Battle of Bloody Mose. More than half of the British invasion force was killed or captured. The rest fled back to the English colonial town of Savannah, Georgia. Fort Mose itself, however, was destroyed in the fighting.

Over the next twelve years, Fort Mose's African community lived within St. Augustine as free and seemingly equal citizens of Spanish Florida. That is, until the Spanish government appointed a new Governor of Florida, Fulgencio Garcia de Solis, an ardent racist and segregationist who in 1752 ordered African citizens of St. Augustine to rebuild Fort Mose on a new site and return there to live. The town and community

---

3   Modibo Kadalie, *Pan-African Social Ecology*, 62–63.

persisted for another decade, until the 1763 Treaty of Paris, in which Spain ceded Florida to the British. At that time, a large number of free African people living in Spanish Florida evacuated to Cuba, including most of the people living in Fort Mose. Others who lived in the many autonomous and multi-racial towns and villages that proliferated throughout Florida chose to remain on the mainland and soon contributed to the development of the emerging Seminole society. The Fort Mose site remained vacant for decades and was eventually destroyed by the British during the War of 1812.

Archeological investigations of Fort Mose began in the late 1980s and have continued intermittently into the twenty-first century. Due to dredging, climate change, and the constantly shifting landscapes of the Atlantic coast, the site of the original Fort Mose is entirely underwater, presenting an obvious archeological challenge. The site of the second Mose is only partially underwater, and excavations continue there as of the time of this writing. Studies of these sites have uncovered a variety of artifacts, including glass beads and bottle shards, fragments of stone metates (Indigenous Mesoamerican tools for processing grain), ceramic pottery of Indigenous design, and ceramic pipe fragments of English origin.[4] In 1994 the area was designated as a historical landmark and now features a museum, boat launch, and a scenic boardwalk from where visitors can look out beyond the tidal salt marsh toward the site of the original settlements.

As we worked together to create this book, Modibo and I often learned new aspects of these histories that sometimes surprised us. Our investigation into the origin of the name "Fort Mose" is one such example. While searching digital archives for colonial-era maps to include in this volume, I happened upon an English-language map of Florida dated 1760, which labeled the settlement "Fort Musa," resembling the common Arabic name for Moses. Another map dated 1763 labeled the same site as "Fort Moosa," which suggests the Arabic pronunciation of the same name. Seeking clarification, I was delighted to encounter Samory Rashid's book, *Black Muslims in the U.S.*, which includes a very brief history of Fort Mose and explains the name as follows:

---

4   As of July 2021, the artifacts listed here are on display at the Fort Mose Historic State Park museum.

> Native Americans and black fugitives were the origi-
> nal inhabitants of the site they appear to have named
> "Moosa." Spain would later rename the site *Garcia* [sic]
> *Real de Santa Teresa de Mose*, a composite of the name
> "Mose" (more accurately, Musa); Garcia [*sic*] Real, the
> king of Spain; and Teresa of Aviles, Spain's patron saint.
> [...]
> The word Musa, which is discussed in the Quran,
> holds special significance for Muslims. It recounts the
> story of Moses and the escape of his followers from
> enslavement under Pharaoh. It is also the story of
> the Jewish Exodus in the Old Testament. For black
> Christians, Muslims, and Jews, the story of Moses
> (*Musa*) holds a special significance not always shared by
> white coreligionists. Despite changes in its contempo-
> rary spelling and pronunciation, seemingly related to its
> renaming by the Spaniards, original documents includ-
> ing those submitted in 1740 by General Oglethorpe
> spell the fort's name the way it is pronounced phoneti-
> cally by Muslims, "Moosa." Upon their return after 1740,
> Oglethorpe's English troops would speak of "bloody
> Moosa."[5]

The revelation that Fort Mose (or Fort Musa) was named by the
inhabitants themselves (many of whom were undoubtedly practicing
Muslims), and that this name—though misinterpreted—was recorded in
both Spanish and English colonial documentation of the period, supports
Kadalie's argument about the settlement's relative autonomy, especially
in its earliest incarnation. Fort Mose was not constructed by the Spanish
colonial administration for the benefit of Africans fleeing slavery in the
English colonies. Instead, Mose was built, settled, named, organized, and
governed by the Africans themselves as part of their collective quest for

---

5   Samory Rashid, *Black Muslims in the U.S.: History, Politics, and the Struggle of a
    Community* (New York: Palgrave Macmillan, 2013), 48–49.

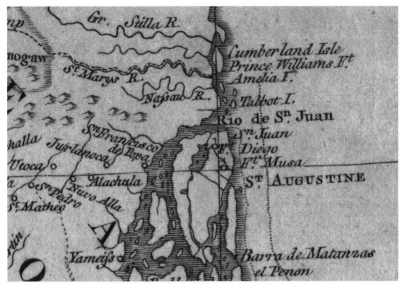

Figure 2. Fort Mose (shown just north of St. Augustine) written as "Fort Musa" on a 1760 map. Other maps of the period read "Fort Moosa."

freedom. Today, the site remains a monument to the tradition of directly democratic Black autonomy in southeastern North America.

Part Three of this book features a transcribed conversation between myself and Dr. Kadalie in which we discuss what lessons activists and academics alike might learn from his study of the Great Dismal Swamp and Fort Mose. The historical examples of intimate direct democracy documented in this book, however, are not prescriptive or prefigurative. Readers expecting a blueprint for revolution or utopian society are sure to find their expectations unfulfilled by this small volume. After all, the Great Dismal Swamp and Fort Mose were not utopias. Not even close. The people who lived in these places were refugees, displaced from their African homelands, living under constant threat of violence, enslavement, or death. But, as Dr. Kadalie demonstrates, their memory challenges our understanding of history itself. In studying these sites of North American maroonage, we discover how the desire for genuinely democratic life-styles, even ecological lifestyles, has been a driving force of social change throughout human history.

In this way, Modibo's account of these histories is ultimately a call for readers to reconsider our understanding of history itself. We must do more than simply acknowledge or remember these histories. We must critically examine how and why they ought to be remembered and continuously revisit them as time passes and as their importance becomes once again illuminated by the freedom struggles of future generations. Critical historiography—the study of how historians' own prejudices and biases have influenced our knowledge of the past—is a political project. It is a revolutionary project. It is an approach to history that reveals and challenges hierarchies and power structures that might otherwise go unnoticed. Since our understanding of the past inspires and informs our vision of possible futures, Kadalie challenges readers and historians to look beyond the reductive narratives of historical elites, statesmen, and charismatic individuals and to instead reinterpret history through the lens of collective social motion.

Perhaps it is Dr. Kadalie's emphasis on critical historiography that most distinguishes this book, highlighting his sensitivity to how the oppressive hierarchies of capitalism, patriarchy, and state power have influenced historians' interpretations of the past. Exposing and correcting these structural academic biases has become an integral part of Modibo's own activism.

As Franz Fanon is remembered for saying, "Each generation must discover its mission, fulfill it or betray it, in relative opactiy."[6] History plays a role in this, as each generation's understanding of the past creates the framework upon which they can design possible futures. As new generations of young activists emerge in the mid-twenty-first century, books like this one offer them a more revolutionary view of the past and their own place in the human quest for freedom that was taken up by their forbears and will be inevitably carried forward by their inheritors.

We also hope this book will inspire readers to rethink their understanding of democracy itself. Democracy, in its most direct and intimate form, has nothing at all to do with the election of representative politicians into a governing body, nor with any form of statecraft. And, of course, democracy has even less to do with the founding of the United

---

6   Franz Fanon, *The Wretched of the Earth* (New York: Grove Press, 2004), 132.

States of America in the late-eighteenth century. As Dr. Kadalie has explained elsewhere:

> Some people think that [the United States of America] is the great experiment in democracy, but there has never been any democracy here. Some people are in love with what they are told America is, but when you look at history very carefully you will find that the people whom I call, "freedom seekers and resisters" were constantly running away from America.
>
> Anyone from Daniel Shays up in Massachusetts, to the slaves who were running south and west to Spanish or Indigenous territory, none of these people wanted to be a part of America. They ran as far as they could, as quickly as they could, and they were creating societies in the process that were more democratic than America ever was, and that is the kind of history that we need to be focusing upon.
>
> [...]
>
> In fact, no freedom-loving person wanted to be a part of the creation of [the United States]. They were quite literally resisting or running away from America. So, history must be re-written from the point of view of these freedom-seeking resisters, not merely as individuals but as an entire freedom movement.[7]

Indeed, far from being a democracy itself, the United States was built by slavery and the genocidal destruction of actually-existing Indigenous and maroon democracies. The Great Dismal Swamp and Fort Mose are only two examples of many such small democracies, including African maroon communities, larger Indigenous societies, and multi-racial communities of people fleeing or resisting European settler colonialism. Maroon communities in particular proliferated in the eras of Spanish colonialism in Florida. Most of these settlements remained necessarily

---

7   Modibo Kadalie, *Pan-African Social Ecology*, 69.

small in order to avoid detection, but there were some maroon communities larger than Fort Mose.

One remarkable example is the community of Angola in western central Florida, which was established near the convergence of the Bradenton and Manatee Rivers from 1812 until 1821. Angola was not nearly as well documented as Fort Mose, but with an estimated population of 600–750 people, it was several times larger. The Angola site was built on or near an Indigenous mound complex; African and Indigenous families in the area shared resources, including fresh water from the Manatee Mineral Spring until many of the areas inhabitants fled to the Bahamas in 1821.[8] Historical and archeological studies of Angola, Florida are still developing and although the site is not discussed in depth in this present book, its story echoes Kadalie's narrative of intimately egalitarian North American maroon societies.

Modibo Kadalie's directly democratic worldview is one rooted in what he often calls the neo-pan-Africanist tradition, which finds its roots in the writings of mid-twentieth-century scholars like Trinidad's CLR James, Guyana's Eusi Kwayana, Jamaica's Joseph Edwards and resonates in the works of Black American revolutionaries like Ella Baker and political prisoners like Mumia Abu Jamal and Lorenzo Kom'boa Ervin. Neo-pan-Africanism, according to Kadalie, is distinguished from classical pan-Africanism by the questions of state power and ecology. Where classical pan-Africanism assumed that freedom for African peoples could be attained through the emergence of African state power, neo-pan-Africanism clarifies that state power itself is inherently oppressive, ecologically destructive, and ultimately counter-intuitive to any genuinely democratic peoples' movements. This neo-pan-Africanist lens is perfectly calibrated for investigating the histories of the Great Dismal Swamp and Fort Mose: two sites in the African diaspora where groups of people cooperated voluntarily and democratically to build communities in which they could defend one another from some of the most horrific oppressions in history. The ability to see history through a horizontalist lens, however, is equally

---

8   Rosalyn Howard, "Looking for Angola: An Archaeological and Ethnohistorical Search for a Nineteenth Century Florida Maroon Community and its Caribbean Connections," *The Florida Historical Quarterly*, Vol. 92, No. 1 (Summer 2013), 32–68.

important outside of the pan-Africanist tradition. In the twenty-first century, historians and archeologists in a diverse array of fields, and especially with regards to the ancient Americas, are becoming more critical of their own blindspots regarding directly democratic societies.[9] In Kadalie's study of Fort Mose, the author makes a considerable effort to contextualize the emergence of the maroon community within the Indigenous history of the southeastern region.

I returned to Fort Mose Historic State Park in July 2021 as part of a small expedition on behalf of the Autonomous Research Institute for Direct Democracy and Social Ecology, an organization founded by Dr. Kadalie in 2017. I was accompanied by my partner, Margo Fortune. We viewed the museum and documentary film, as I had done with Modibo years earlier. We also examined the museum's ambitious plans to build a full-scale replica of Fort Mose on the state park grounds. During our visit, we launched a kayak from the floating dock behind the museum and paddled out into the salt marsh toward the small island that now sits at the site of the second Fort Mose (1752–1763). No trace of the settlement remains above ground, but we could see tents and markers indicating an ongoing archeological excavation.

It is exciting to wonder what new insights might be gleaned from this and future studies. What might newly uncovered artifacts reveal to us about North American maroonage once we consider Modibo Kadalie's critical reappraisal of these earliest underground railroads and their

---

9   For example, in a recent archeological study of Aguada Fénix, an ancient Mayan cultural center established circa 1000 BCE, archeologist Takeshi Inomata argues "we don't see the evidence of the presence of powerful elites" in the construction of the site's large buildings and monuments. According to Inomata: "It's not just hierarchical social organization with the elite that makes monuments like this possible. ... This kind of understanding gives us important implications about human capability, and the potential of human groups. You may not necessarily need a well-organized government to carry out these kinds of huge projects. People can work together to achieve amazing results." See: NSF Public Affairs, "Largest, oldest Maya monument suggests importance of communal work," National Science Foundation (18 June 2020). https://www.nsf.gov/discoveries/disc_summ.jsp?cntn_id=300785. See also: T. Inomata, D. Triadan, V.A. Vázquez López, et al., "Monumental architecture at Aguada Fénix and the rise of Maya civilization," *Nature* 582 (2020), 530–533.

Figure 3. Archeological excavation of the second Fort Mose (1752-1763). Photograph by Andrew Zonneveld, July 2021.

relationship to ecology and state power? And what more might we come to understand about the directly democratic possibilities of present and future freedom movements?

Such questions demonstrate the radical potential of history to challenge our worldview and inspire change. By reframing our image of the past, we remind each other of our collective revolutionary power. Throughout human history, ordinary people—the poor, the marginalized, the working class, or even the enslaved—have never needed saviors or heroes as they fought to abolish oppressive systems and to create new worlds on their own authority. Not only are oppressed peoples capable of liberating and governing themselves, but their forms of self-government that have emerged throughout history also point the way toward an ecological future in which directly democratic human communities can live in harmony with one another and with the rest of the natural world.

Historical movements of Black autonomy in places like Georgia, Florida, and South Carolina have largely been ignored by historians, and as surprising as it may seem, this is equally true of radical or left-wing historians, who we might usually expect to take a keen interest in such histories. In the sparse instances when these stories have been studied, they have often been misunderstood, as has the ecological history of the region.[10] While many scholars and activists seemingly regard the region as backward and forgettable, Dr. Kadalie describes the swamps, woods, and wetlands of the southeastern Atlantic coast as an area overflowing with life and radical possibilities.

This book is the first to offer a directly democratic perspective on North American maroonage while simultaneously placing those stories in their proper ecological and Indigenous social contexts. Readers who are unfamiliar with the region may be surprised at the depth and complexity of political and social history of this region, but in the twenty-first century we can no longer afford to avoid learning about the South. As one of the most ethnically diverse, ecologically diverse, and economically poor regions of North America, the Southeast exists on the frontlines of the struggle against racism, climate change, and capitalism. Modibo Kadalie's comparative study of the Great Dismal Swamp and Fort Mose digs at the historical roots of those struggles and is an invaluable text for anyone who chooses to take up the work of building a better world.

10　A noteworthy exception to this rule can be found in Neal Shirley and Saralee Stafford's impressive volume, *Dixie Be Damned: 500 Years of Insurrection in the American South* (Oakland: AK Press, 2015).

ACKNOWLEDGMENTS

We would like to thank everyone who helped make this book possible, especially Dr. Janis Coombs Reid, for offering notes on every draft of the manuscript and for graciously assisting with proofreading. We would also like to thank Megan Leach for designing the book cover and Margo Summer Fortune for creating one of the maps used in this volume.

Many thanks, as well, to everyone who read Dr. Kadalie's previous volume, *Pan-African Social Ecology: Speeches, Conversations, and Essays* (2019). We hope that this new book will help to deepen those conversations that were started almost three years ago in what now seems, in some ways, like an entirely different period of history.

—Modibo Kadalie and Andrew Zonneveld, 2022.

PREFACE

The history of any oppressive society cannot be written from the commanding heights of the oppressors themselves. In order to be accurate, it must be written from the perspective of those whom they oppress at the bottom of society. This volume is offered as a small contribution to the urgent and necessary task of collectively rewriting the social history of the Americas. Almost everything that is currently found in print—from the shortest brochure to the thickest encyclopedic volume—extolls the virtue of the grand experiment that is the United States' "democracy." Even where we find criticism of this society's many flaws, these are quickly dismissed as correctable if only we would honestly engage in a meaningful discussion of its weaknesses. The fallacious story purports that these flaws were not germane to democratic U.S. ideals as they were conceived, but that they have only emerged from the imperfect attempt at the implementation of these ideals. This unfortunate failure, as the story continues, is blamed on those few corrupt individuals who simply did not understand the true exceptional purity of the U.S. democratic creed.

The idea that the owners of the brutal profiteering agricultural enslavement farms that originated in the southeastern coastal region of North America could be remembered as the venerated founders of a society that boasts itself as the "leader of the free world" is preposterous on its dirty face. From its very beginning, an endemic system of privilege has dominated the written record and social practices of the early colonial American landscape. This system found root in all manner of elitism and hierarchy, containing a pervasive and rabidly infectious patriarchy and vile white supremacy baked into its institutional fabric. As it evolved, it became a complex international commercial system that formed the basis of modern capitalism through the genocidal destruction of Native peoples, the aggressive confiscation of their lands, and the disruption of their social-ecological development. This occurred in parallel with the systematic theft and translocation of enormous numbers of skilled African laborers which occasioned the violent dismemberment of the social-ecological development on the entire continent of Africa.

In the Americas, colonial invaders from Europe encountered thriving human societies that were mostly devoid of rigid hierarchies. These societies were, for the most part, in ecological harmony with the dynamic array of organic life within which they lived. These people had organized themselves into intimate and autonomous social formations that could be regarded as directly democratic, much as the kidnapped and trafficked African laborers had done in their own homelands. The Great Dismal Swamp and Fort Mose are two sites where these truly democratic histories of the Atlantic world converged in their opposition to European and U.S. settler colonialism.

At first glance, these two sites may seem to be places with little in common. One is a vast natural landscape filled with plant and animal life. The other is a compact, human-built social and political space. What they both have in common, however, is that they were places of refuge, places where those who were seeking sanctuary from the wretchedness and dehumanizing imprisonment of enslaved labor sought to create free living spaces where they could be their most fulfilling selves, living in harmony with each other and with the rest of the natural world.

This work attempts to give full consideration to the social-ecological organization of Indigenous and enslaved African inhabitants of the Great Dismal Swamp and Fort Mose as they resisted the violent imposition of the earliest forms of capitalism. In so doing they were able to create (along with some dispossessed Europeans in their midst who were also being exploited) new forms of intimate social relations that we are just now beginning to understand.

This new history must be written from the perspective of the African maroons of the swamp, the Seminoles of the riverbanks, and the piney woods "crackers" of the upcountry pine barrows. They are not ghostly shadowy figures blankly peering at us from some distant place separated from each other and from us. They were people of distinctive origins, unified and locked in a struggle against the frightening, undemocratic, and inhuman United States of America, which they witnessed coming into being before their eyes. Although they have been gone for centuries, these people still have something to tell us and we have much to learn from them. Upon introducing ourselves to these freedom-seekers, we discover that they are us and we are they, as we live and struggle within our own times. Our history is not a story of unrecognized contributions to the greatness of U.S. "democracy," or that of any other nation-state. Our history is one part of a broader human struggle to dismantle nation states entirely and to create more directly democratic institutions that are compatible with and integrated into a more socially ecological world.

This book tells the story of how and when we have met each other as oppressed peoples in the racist and hierarchical settler colonies of North America. As we have become companions in the human quest for freedom, we have come to more fully realize that we are fellow travelers. Good morning and hello. We have a lot to do. It may take a while.

— Modibo Kadalie, 2022.

PROSPECTUS

The following is a conceptual effort to contextualize the struggle for self-organized, autonomous eco-communities of Indigenous peoples and formerly-enslaved, self-emancipated Africans as an independent democratic force within the contestations between the British and Spanish colonial empires in the region that eventually became known as the southeastern United States. This period in history was characterized by a protracted war of genocidal displacement against the network of Indigenous eco-communities in North America and the Caribbean by distinctively hostile alien settlements controlled by ascendant social classes that had originated within the emerging capitalist nation states of western Europe. This ongoing war of attrition, resistance, and ecological devastation continues into the twenty-first century.

We will be using the historical examples of Fort Mose in Spanish-held Florida prior to 1780 and the Great Dismal Swamp in the British settler colonies in what is now the North American states of Virginia and North Carolina during a preceding period.

First, we will begin to scratch the surface of the erroneous assumptions that underpin most, if not all, of the dominant historiography surrounding these sites. Then we will attempt to firmly establish the nature of their origin. Thereafter, we will try to demonstrate the general purpose that these assumptions serve. Then we will critically examine many of the specific misconceptions that are derived from these fallacious ideas and notions.

We will do this by asserting the real meaning of the communities of Fort Mose and the Great Dismal Swamp as places of defiance, resistance, freedom, and ecologically symbiotic intimacy. We will attempt to integrate these conceptions within our narrative as it unfolds.

Our general sequence of exposition will begin with a consideration of the Great Dismal Swamp, a very important and contested natural space. This place of refuge is only now, in the twenty-first century, being acknowledged as having played a crucial yet obscure role in the proliferation of many self-emancipated maroon communities as the genocidal conquest of North America unfolded with devastating consequences. From there, we will look south to Spanish-occupied Florida in the eighteenth century, where a self-organized and free African town, Fort Mose, stood at the center of a conflict between two empires.

During the course of the events discussed in this work, we will also sadly see the emergence of a new empire—the United States—which emerged during this period of colonial contestation. In contrast to the Spanish and British empires, this new fledgling U.S. empire was distinguished from its outset by a bogus democracy set up to encourage and empower the brutal and inhuman profiteers of slave labor farms.

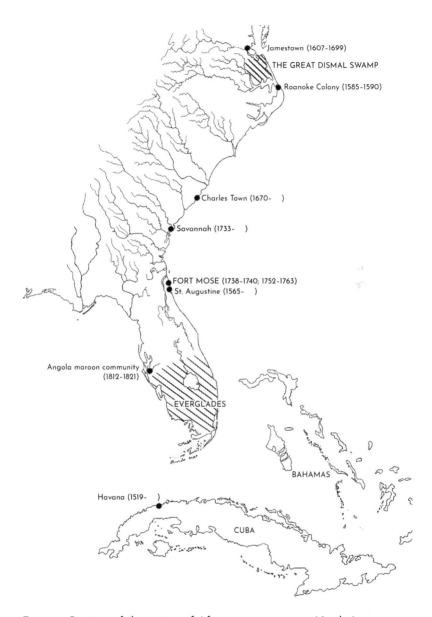

Figure 4. Position of three sites of African maroonage in North America—the Great Dismal Swamp, Fort Mose, and Florida's Angola community—in relation to major European colonial centers. Illustrated by Margo Summer Fortune, January 2022.

Part One:
The Great Dismal Swamp

CHAPTER 1.
THE GREAT DISMAL SWAMP AND ITS SOCIAL-ECOLOGICAL CONTEXT

The area we know as the Great Dismal Swamp was (and is) an expansive marshy wetland landscape in the middle of a region that was conquered by settlers from England beginning in the early seventeenth century, after several earlier attempts by Spanish missionaries and plunderers to exploit the wealth of the region for the Spanish crown, beginning almost a full century before permanent English settlement. Only a very small fragment still exists of this huge, majestic, evolving and interconnected network of ecosystems, which have by now been ravaged by cash-crop agriculture and its devastating social-ecological effects for nearly five hundred years.

This mid-Atlantic coastal swamp is today found astride the boundaries of what we now consider northeastern North Carolina and southeastern Virginia. In 1973 what remained of this unique network of ecological systems was officially designated as the "Great Dismal Swamp National Wildlife Refuge" by the United States Fish and Wildlife Service and includes more than 175 square miles (112,000 acres) of wetlands containing a substantial section of old growth forest that surrounds a 3,100-acre natural lake. That is the way it remains today in 2022, with almost ninety percent of the original swampland now destroyed and the rest languishing in a decimated state, bearing little resemblance to its earlier existence. Prior to European contact, the Great Dismal Swamp occupied an area greater than 1,200,000 acres, stretching from what is now Suffolk, Virginia on the north to Edenton, North Carolina on the south. The remaining 175 square miles nevertheless represents a core of an even larger zone of social-ecological evolutionary history, both before and after the coming of Europeans settlers.[1]

The Great Dismal Swamp is part of a greater natural zone that once stretched from the swamps just south of Suffolk continuing south to include both sides of what is now the Albemarle Sound and the rivers and streams that empty into it. It involved the regions to the south and southeast of the Sound, known to locals as the Alligator and the Pocosin Swamps, extending as far south to the area that is today called, "the East Dismal Swamp," immediately north of the Pamlico River. It is clear that this massive bioregion, though now fragmented beyond recognition, has offered a dazzling array of ecological possibilities for the inhabitants who lived and thrived there for many thousands of years. It also provides an ecological back drop for the history of Indigenous and African maroon resistance to capitalist colonial expansion along the southeastern Atlantic seaboard.

In order to bring even greater geo-ecological context to the history of the region, our understanding of the Great Dismal Swamp must be conceptually enlarged to include the connecting marshlands, bogs, and the necklace of barrier islands that extend from the Chesapeake Bay southward along the Atlantic coast all the way to the greater Florida Everglades (as it existed then)—as well as the coastal plains that stretch inland, adjacent to this chain of connecting ecosystems—all exposed as one of the abiding legacies of the last Ice Age. All of this natural living abundance was peopled in a rich tapestry of intimate, directly democratic social formations creatively sustaining themselves in harmony with the rest of nature and following their own interdependent patterns of development.

While such regions have been inhabited throughout human history, they were deemed useless by European colonizers during the initial phase of exploration and settlement. In fact, these swamps and forests were in many ways a hindrance to the expansion of capitalist monocrop agriculture and even to European habitation (at least at first). To the colonizers, the Great Dismal Swamp was a wild place unsuitable for settlement or

---

1   North Carolina Division of Parks and Recreation of the Department of Natural and Cultural Resources, "History Highlights," *Dismal Swamp State Park*, n.d., https://www.ncparks.gov/dismal-swamp-state-park/history.

farming, located between the first two English settlements of Roanoke Island and Jamestown. Interestingly, neither of these colonial settlements survived for very long. Nor has any city of significant size developing in the bioregional zone of what is now eastern North Carolina to this day. Clearly, there were many real natural challenges that limited capitalist agricultural expansion in this unique region.

In the "new world," the swamp became both an evolving metaphor and a living geophysical place. The story of this region represents a clash of opposing ecological perspectives. The descriptor of "dismal" reveals the attitude of colonialists toward the ecology of the region they had invaded. For European explorers, and most especially for colonial settlers—with their deadly diseases, their violent disregard for the natural world, and their enslaved-labor farming system (the plantation system)—the swamp was indeed a dark and foreboding place. These settlers had a very different conception of the natural world than the Algonquian-speaking inhabitants of the region or the African maroons that found refuge in places like this. To the aliens from across the sea, this was indeed a "new world," a world to be dominated; a place to be tamed, subjugated, and subdued; a place to establish their way of life, their "civilization," and to extend the dominion of their patriarchal monotheistic religion. Most of all, it was a place to be bent to their purposes and exploited for their benefit. The dismal swamps stood in their way.

To Indigenous peoples and enslaved Africans who were witnessing the wanton and ignorant destruction of all things natural, including human institutions of intimate self-governance, the swamp was a place of peace and of refuge from those frightful European conquerors. After all, the Great Dismal Swamp had been populated for thousands of years. It was a wonderous place, often filled with challenges and crises and yet a quietly beautiful place to those who appreciated its natural grandeur. Only hostile conquerors, who simply could not comprehend how humanity could be integrated harmoniously with the rest of nature, regarded the swamp as a troubled place in which humans could not prosper.

The swamp was a place full of life and astonishing possibility, but in an ecosystem such as this one, growing and evolving so constantly and rapidly—almost aggressively—archeological evidence of human eco-communities and their connections to the environment have been almost completely erased.[2] Prior to the coming of European settlers, there is no (yet revealed) evidence that any huge ancient stone or even wooden monuments ever existed within this larger region. There are no remains of feudal castles that speak to the raw vanity of social hierarchy; no great markers of bloody battles that reveal the brutality of conflicting armies driven by the greed of sovereigns or other hierarchically organized social formations. There are no existing records of mighty kings, chiefs, potentates, or individual tyrants that reveal the rabid individualism or egomania that is conjured up and celebrated by elitist historians. Indeed, there is little or no evidence of the existence of any sort of hierarchical social organization here prior to its violent introduction by European intrusion. Yet we must never forget that the Great Dismal Swamp has supported human social habitation for thousands of years.

Hints of still-unexplored human communities of the past can still be discovered languishing within the acidic muck of this seemingly insignificant place. Such dynamic and complex ecosystems as these—both large and small—defy capitalistic exploitation and destruction, allowing our planet to go on living. In a real sense, the lifeforms that continue to strive in places like the Great Dismal Swamp represent nature standing in the way of the raw capitalist exploitation that rips the heart and soul out of those natural places of the earth where humans have been welcomed into a more harmonious and symbiotic social-ecological integration.

OTHER LARGER ECOSYSTEMS

After thousands of years, even now there are still certain unique natural landscapes which defy fences, survey stakes, or physical markers of individual, corporate, or even state ownership or control. These places are not untouched, unexplored, or in any way mysterious. They represent the prolific legacy of the previous ice age, which reveals itself in many different and unique ways. Misunderstood and unappreciated, they resist exploitation and remain relatively intact because they simply refuse to be

---

2   Murray Bookchin defines eco-communities as communities that are "conceived to be part of the balance of nature ... with an active sense of participation in the overall environment and the cycles of nature." See Murray Bookchin, *The Ecology of Freedom: The Emergence and Dissolution of Hierarchy* (Oakland: AK Press, 2005), 112.

destroyed. They have defied attempts at their commoditization even as components of their biomes have been severed or extracted. Some such places have even reemerged from a residual fragment of their former selves to reassert a degree of sustainability and lay claim to their place within the Earth's dynamic network of living ecosystems.

These expansive yet remote landscapes on the southeastern coast of North America were usually swamps or hammocks within marshy plains or exposed as barrier islands, each demonstrating some distinctive character, one from the other. They are still found all over the southeastern United States, taking many different (though greatly diminished) forms and are today designated by names such as the Great Dismal Swamp,[3] the Everglades,[4] the Atchafalaya basin, and the Okefenokee Swamp, among others. Further inland, beyond the coastal plains and piedmont, mountains offered similar refuge from increasingly more violent European conquest in their centuries-long colonial expansion. These were natural places where Indigenous peoples thrived and self-emancipated Africans found refuge, and each created intimate and directly democratic eco-communities. These communities were also havens for some Europeans who sought a more liberating form of social existence.

As early as the seventeenth century, documented self-organized eco-communities of formally enslaved people lived within the confines of the great swamps. The emergence of these maroon communities coincided

---

3   In 1763 a profit-making enterprise called "the Adventurers for Draining the Dismal Swamp" was created by none other than George Washington, along with other monied interests from Virginia, to build causeways and canals to drain the swamp and make it usable for commercial exploitation. The first efforts failed but successive attempts did initiate the process of reducing the swamp to its present diminished state.

4   As early as 1850 the U.S. federal government began its assault on the greater Everglades with the passage of the Swamp and Overflowed Lands Act of 1850. At that point in time, the greater Everglades extended up to and around Lake Okeechobee. It has been decimated and now only barely resembles its former self. For a detailed description of the governmental policies that led to the actual draining of the Everglades see: Clay J. Landry, "Who Drained the Everglades," *Property and Environment Research Center*, Vol. 20, No. 1, (Spring 2002).

almost exactly with the spread of the infamous enslaved-labor farming system, which became known as the "planation" system.[5]

The great swamps, in many ways, represent the other great natural places on the planet in microcosm. Though their bio-diversity is different in almost every detail, their nourishment of our living planet presents a common theme. We are only now beginning to understand, through an informed and sensitive social-ecological scientific orientation, the profound character and essence of these critically important natural places. They are disappearing, but not merely disappearing. They are being destroyed by exploitative capitalist industry and the catastrophic climate change it has caused. The great Amazon basin;[6] the great jungled belt of equatorial Africa; the Gangu wetlands of Uganda; the thick jungles of Borneo and Sumatra are all tragic examples of this continuing catastrophe. Unique land and water systems like these support the greatest landed biodiversity on earth. Such places are the result of naturally occurring planetary climate changes interacting with the bio-geological changes of the earth over time and contribute to the well-being of all life on Earth. Even in the face of widespread systemic destruction, they remain defiant. In so doing, they keep humanity alive. We will not "save" places such as these. If we are to be saved, they will save us.

---

5   American University, "Freedom in the Swamp: Unearthing the secret history of the Great Dismal Swamp," *ScienceDaily*. www.sciencedaily.com/releases/2011/05/110516075940.htm.

6   Erin Blakemore, "Amazon Jungle Once Home to Millions More Than Previously Thought," *National Geographic*, 27 March 2018. https://www.nationalgeographic.com/history/article/amazon-jungle-ancient-population-satellite-computer-model.

CHAPTER 2.
THE PEOPLE OF
THE GREAT SWAMPS

By 1,000 BCE the Indigenous woodland culture was beginning to establish itself in and around the region that would later become known as coastal North Carolina and Virginia. Following a pattern of settlement along the rivers and streams, they practiced a hybrid style of hunting, fishing, and gathering mixed with some agriculture. They grew squash and gourds, along with beans; later, around 200 BCE, they began to grow corn. Their eco-communities became larger, more numerous, and more autonomous with respect to each other, giving rise to a greater degree of cultural diversity and, ironically, more economic interdependence. Within smaller communities, identity was based upon kinship and a common understanding of their origin as affirmed in creation myths and maintained in the lore that was passed from one generation to the next as part of a rich oral tradition. As these communities began to spread and become more numerous their sense of shared identity grew to be based upon a common tribe. Tribal identity introduced a wider and more diverse understanding of not only the individual and group self-identity, but also that of others with whom they acknowledged as having a shared identity. Paradoxically, this diversity led to the beginnings of cultural exchanges, which in turn led to a greater degree of common cultural identity.

One of the ways that this diversification can be traced is through language. There were essentially three major linguistic groupings that had evolved in the zone of the greater swamp region by the seventeenth century: Algonquian, Iroquois, and Siouan. The Algonquian-speaking clans lined the eastern coast of North America, stretching from the mouth of the Cape Fear River in the south to the present-day Canadian Maritime provinces of New Brunswick, Prince Edward Island, and Nova Scotia on both sides of the Saint Lawrence River to the north.

The Iroquois speakers were inland in both North Carolina and Virginia and extended north into Pennsylvania and into central New York along the southern banks of Lake Ontario. There they developed a complex and intricate governing system known as the Haudenosaunee Confederacy. This highly organized and politically flat system of "democracy" was initially composed of five distinctive cultural groupings: the Mohawk, Onondaga, Oneida, Cayuga, and the Seneca. The Tuscarora would join them later, after they were forced to migrate from what is now North Carolina to north-central Pennsylvania and south-central New York. Interestingly the Cherokees of the North Carolina, Tennessee, and Georgia mountains spoke a variation of Iroquois. There are two influential theories in this regard. The first simply claims that the Cherokee originated in the area of Pennsylvania and New York and separated from the main body of the Iroquois-speaking peoples and migrated southward through the Shenandoah into Western North Carolina, Tennessee, and North Georgia. The other theory says that the main body of the Iroquois originated from the large urban complex of Cahokia, a major urban population center located on the eastern banks of the confluence of the Missouri and the Mississippi rivers. The Iroquois left Cahokia and moved northeast. Sometime during their long journey, they separated into two groups. One group went north into the Lake Ontario area and the other went east into the mountains of Appalachia and became known as the Cherokee.[1] Both theories account for the linguistic similarity.

The Siouan languages were spoken in central North Carolina and into Virginia. Elements and dialects of this group can be found in the Midwest and in the great plains into Canada.

---

1   We will discuss Cahokia in greater depth in Part Two of this volume, but it is worth noting here the persistence of an ancient Cherokee legend of the Aníkutáni, an ancient and abusive authoritarian regime that was violently overthrown by its underclasses. It is entirely possible that the Aní-kutáni legend was inspired by historical events and may hint at an explanation for the fall of Cahokia and may support the theory of Cherokee origins at Cahokia. See: David Graeber and David Wengrow, *The Dawn of Everything: A New History of Humanity* (New York: Farrar, Strauss, and Grioux, 2021), 472. (A.Z)

This evolving set of common yet distinctive languages, dialects, and mutually intelligible verbal expressions are indicators of a certain degree of sustained social intercourse within and between these socially dynamic networks. We would be hard pressed to call it "trade," to the degree and intensity that it occurs in a modern capitalist society. It was, nevertheless, a sustained cultural exchange throughout an amalgam of self-governing and relatively autonomous societies that allowed literally hundreds of thousands of people to live and prosper collectively in unity with nature. For the most part, people in these societies believed in the harmonious unity of all of the components of the natural world, including themselves. People belonged to nature, not the other way around. No aspect of nature could possibly belong to any individual. Nature, therefore, could not be divided and sold as the private property of any person or group.

Despite the descriptions of many ignorant European scholars both then and now, Indigenous peoples did not live in "chaos." Chaos, in fact, was introduced with the coming of European settlers and the practice of private ownership of land and other means needed by communities for their social-ecological sustainability. This form of social organization, in which production exists to sustain for-profit exploitative exchange, requires a social hierarchy with non-laboring benefactors accumulating and hoarding nearly all of a society's wealth. Any form of genuinely collective or egalitarian social existence in harmony with the rest of the natural world would be incompatible with such a regime.

The layout of Native villages and their shared collective living spaces indicated a communal way of life. Land cultivation was collective; food stores were held in common; hunting and gathering took place in a cooperative manner, and collectively produced goods were allocated along equitable principles. There is no evidence of any privately controlled social assets. All of this is demonstrative of a relatively flat, non-hierarchical social structure. The presence of any form of nobility, under these circumstances, was a figment of hierarchical and elitist European imaginations.

Along with this shared communal life came shared responsibility and a shared system of collective decision making and governance. The democratic decision making of the Haudenosaunee Confederacy is well known, but many other Native peoples in North America had developed even more democratic lifestyles. Doubtless, a critical study of the many and varied forms of non-hierarchal governance of Indigenous peoples prior to the devastating impact of European invasion would reveal many lessons in direct social-ecological symbiosis. This is the unexamined and ignored legacy of Indigenous history in the coastal regions of southeastern North America prior to the decimation of their social-ecological institutions by European invasion.

In the densely populated area of coastal Virginia and North Carolina, where the earliest English settlements were established, the coming of the Europeans hit Indigenous populations like a series of social seismic shocks and was a complete disruption of the region's evolving social ecology. The particular set of eco-communities that first encountered the invading settlers were united as the Algonquian-speaking Powhatan Confederacy.[2] From 1610 to 1646, Powhatan communities were decimated by war and disease and many were forced to leave the area.[3] Some of those who remained were enslaved, while others were assimilated into neighboring Native populations further to the north, west, or to the south.[4] Some of these displaced Indigenous communities reconstituted themselves into smaller groups that continued to live along the rivers and streams and in remote regions of the Great Dismal Swamp, beyond the reaches of those violent and disease-ridden intruders with such strange and unnatural customs, who dressed all in black, never laughed, rarely bathed, and who treated all women with disrespect.

THE MARAUDING SPANISH

There is a critical distinction that must be made between the strategy and the motivation of early Spanish and English exploration and

---

2   The "Powhatan," or "the people of the river," were subdivided into the Arrohateck, the Appamattuck, the Pamunkey, The Mattaponi, the Chiskiack, and later the Kecoughtan. The name of the later sub-clan phonetically sounds like the "Croatan" which many believe to have absorbed the lost colony of Roanoke.

3   Joshua J. Mark, "Anglo-Powhatan Wars," *World History Encyclopedia*, 25 February 2021. https://www.worldhistory.org/Anglo-Powhatan_Wars.

4   Native and indentured European labor was used to expand the production of tobacco during this period. Enslaved African labor would be introduced in the area by 1619.

settlement in the Americas. This difference can be found within the changing dynamics of social and economic hierarchies at the respective cores of each European empire. In the case of Spain, explorers were incentivized and patronized by a strong nobility and a rigid class hierarchy reinforced by the Catholic Church. These colonialists, who were the first Europeans to arrive in the region, sought the direct extraction of gold and silver and to convert the Indigenous "heathens" to Catholicism.

Then came the English settlers, who were subsidized by investors in joint stock companies, which indicated a shifting economic hierarchy and a challenge to the English nobility by an ascending merchant and commercial class seeking to establish and sustain profit-making enterprises in the "new world." These joint stock companies provided a mechanism for the accumulation of raw capital in the form of a massive network of enslaved-labor farms (called "plantations") well beyond the political reach of the European aristocracy, a process that eventually led to the socially and ecologically disastrous Industrial Revolution. Indeed, rising merchant classes in England charted an independent course in their political ascendency, a trajectory which was autonomous from the old landed aristocracy and was reinforced by newly emerging social structures and ideas embodied within the various new Protestant denominations of the Christian religion. As we will see, this distinction made all the difference.

After much conflict, war, and continuing contestation between various European empires, these two principal antagonists came to define the character of long-term exploration and settlement in the western hemisphere. The Spanish explorers preceded the English in the region by about fifty years. They established and attempted to maintain a chain of missions from as far north as St. Elena in what is now South Carolina south along the Atlantic coast to St. Augustine.[5] This period of missionary settlement began in 1568 and ended in 1684, when the last of the missions north of St. Augustine were abandoned.[6] The Spanish had been active along the Atlantic coast for almost forty years before any significant settlement or contestation by the English in the region could be seen.

---

5   See 1935 map of the Spanish colonial missions by John Tate Lanning and Willis Physioc.

6   John E. Worth, "Spanish Missions," *New Georgia Encyclopedia*, 8 June 2017. https://www.georgiaencyclopedia.org/articles/arts-culture/spanish-missions.

Figure 5. Map of the Spanish missions of Georgia by John Tate Lanning and Willis Physioc, 1935. According to the Georgia Historical Society, current research on the locations of Spanish missions may refute some of the work presented in this map. Imprecise locations not withstanding, this map successfully illustrates the proliferation of Spanish missions in the region.

The Spanish made no secret of the fact that they were in a feverishly driven search for gold and silver. They mapped almost every river leading inland, up and down the Atlantic coast. They organized long overland treks into the interior, spreading death through disease and wanton killing as part of their campaign of murderous plunder among the Indigenous populations. From their base at St. Elena, they raided the North Carolina and southeastern Virginia coasts, abducting Native women and children and selling them into slavery in Europe, the Caribbean, Central America, and South America.

The Spanish were accompanied on these exploratory voyages by professional soldiers and sailors of African heritage. These individuals were not enslaved, but free. Many were racially mixed and had been born in Spain or Northwest Africa. Others were conscripts captured at sea by raiding ships carrying enslaved people or from landed forays in the new world for laborers to be used in the homes, mines, or the various other schemes aimed at satisfying the greed of the Spanish crown. Some were from autonomous maroon communities in the Caribbean islands or from the mainland of northern South America.

An extensive network of Catholic missions facilitated this exploitative endeavor with catastrophic genocidal consequences for Indigenous populations throughout the entire hemisphere. As this deadly process unfolded, many Indigenous peoples fled inland, away from the approaching Spaniards, and took refuge in places very much like the Great Dismal Swamp. There were many outright revolts against the Spanish missionaries, as part of the overall defensive strategy that Indigenous people adopted in the face of overwhelming and widespread social devastation.

THE ENGLISH COMETH

As early as 1586 Spanish hegemony in the new world was being seriously challenged. At first, English colonists had been motivated by an intense search for gold and silver, much like the Spanish and other European colonial powers, but their focus had gradually shifted toward the production and sale of agricultural cash crops.

Independent pirates as well as state-sponsored privateers had been intercepting Spanish cargo along the trans-Atlantic and Caribbean shipping lanes since the early days of the sixteenth century. They would commandeer any cargo on the high seas, using any method at their disposal. Among the state-sponsored privateers, who played a critical role in the early conflict between the Spanish and the English, was the English privateer Sir Frances Drake. To the Spanish he was a dangerous pirate. To the English crown, he was a brave hero, a celebrated fleet commander in many naval battles against the Spanish, and the first Englishman to circumnavigate the world.[7]

Drake is important to us because in 1586, on a leg of the return voyage of the fleet under his command, he brought approximately seven hundred "cimarrons," (runaway enslaved people seeking refuge from Spanish oppression), the majority of whom were of African heritage, to the region near Roanoke Island and released them as a reward for their loyal service to the Crown.[8] They had served in his campaigns against the Spanish in the Caribbean and along the Spanish Main.[9] On this same voyage, Drake evacuated the survivors of the failed first Roanoke colony, which had been settled only one year earlier in 1585, and took them back to England. A second Roanoke colony was attempted in 1587 and was found abandoned three years later by a resupply party in 1590. What happen to this colony

---

7   Arwin Smallwood, "Tri-Racial Identity of Tuscarora, Meherrin, Melungeon and Other Native Americans in North Carolina, Virginia and East to West," *The Michael Eure Show Podcast,* 17 December 2020. https://www.waketech.edu/student-services/student-advocacy/podcasts/michael-eure-show/tri-racial-identity-tuscarora-meherrin

8   The origin of the word "cimarron" is widely debated, but it is most likely derived from a Taino word, "simaran," meaning "the flight of an arrow." This is generally agreed be the origin of the words "maroon" and "Seminole" to describe frontier societies of self-emancipated Africans, Indigenous peoples, and other runaways in English and Spanish colonial territories respectively. Later, Seminoles would be officially designated a "Native American Tribe" covered by the Indian Removal Act of 1830, which was used to remove all Native Americans to lands west of the Mississippi River. This cleared the way for a massive extension and expansion of enslaved-labor cotton farming during the period from 1825 to 1861. See: Charles C. Mann, *1493: Uncovering the New World Columbus Created* (New York: Alfred A. Knopf, 2011), 331.

9   Among the notable engagements during this voyage were: The Battle of Santo Domingo (1586); the Battle of Cartagena de Indias (8–11 February 1586); the Raid on St. Augustine (27–29 May 1586).

has been the subject of much speculation. The inhabitants of the settlement simply disappeared leaving only the word "Croatan" chiseled in a tree near the compound.[10] This second failed effort at the establishment of a permanent English settlement has become known as "the Lost Colony of Roanoke."[11]

It would not be until 1607 that a different group of English colonialists would arrive on a narrow strip of land in the James River, north of the previous failed settlement. The tenuous colony of Jamestown, financed and supported by the investors of the Virginia Company of London and named for the English king, was established in this location in April of that year. The native Powhatan inhabitants called the area Tsenacomoco and were justifiably fearful of these new intruders based upon their disastrous prior contact with both the Spanish and English. In response to the establishment of Jamestown, they began to expand their limited confederation into a more widely united alliance.

Wahunsenacawh, so-called "chief" of the central village that became known as Powhatan, is misunderstood by most historians. Powhatan was the nucleus of six other eco-communities: Arrohateck, Appamattuck, Pamunkey, Mattaponi, and Chiskiack. While some historians refer to Wahunsenacawh as an "emperor" or as "Powhatan" himself, or as paramount chief and ruler of the Powhatan people, this important figure was more like an administrator or a coordinator of anti-colonial resistance as the Powhatan Confederacy was expanded from the original six to more than thirty villages, in order to mount a more unified opposition in the face of European aggression. In fact, the central village itself was moved more than three times, further and further from the reach of colonial incursion. In this way, Wahunsenacawh can be seen as one of many Indigenous historical figures who influenced the nature of anti-colonial resistance in his time, much like Hiawatha, Tecumseh, Osceola, Crazy Horse, Geronimo, and others in their own times.

For a brief period of time, the English colonists and the Powhatan Confederacy were able to establish a limited trading relationship. As a

---

10   "Croatan" may refer to Kecoughtan, the name of a nearby Powhatan society who may have absorbed the colonists.

11   Karen Ordahl Kupperman, *Roanoke: The Abandoned Colony*, (Lanham: Rowman and Littlefield, 1984).

result, the Jamestown colony was able to survive the winter of 1607–1608 with the supplies that they already had, along with some small amount of trade from Powhatan communities. Because the supplies from Europe were delayed by the time of the colony's second winter in 1609–1610, the people of the colony were literally starving. They actually began preparations to give up and return to England, but the supply ship eventually did arrive and the abandonment of the settlement was averted.

The neighboring Powhatan people were well-prepared and knew how to live through the winters of the region using the natural environment to support them. Yet the more "advanced" European settlers within the same ecological context were resorting, quite literally, to eating their pets and to cannibalism after having lived in the area for a year and a half. Only thirty-eight colonists out of 144 survived that winter, even though they were routinely receiving and stealing food from the neighboring Indigenous communities.

CHAPTER 3.
EUROPEAN SETTLEMENT AND ECOLOGICAL DEGRADATION

The predatory behavior of the colonists toward Indigenous peoples led to increased friction and open warfare. What came to be referred to as the "First Anglo-Powhatan War" (1609-1614) might in fact be more accurately remembered as the beginning of the protracted Powhatan war of resistance. This period of hostility ended temporarily with the inaccurately romanticized and well-known strategic marriage of convenience between John Rolf and a respected Powhatan woman remembered as "Pocahontas." Indeed, a brief period of relative calm allowed the English colony to grow and export some profitable tobacco using both Indigenous and indentured labor. This set them upon a lucrative path that defined the long-term character of the colony and insured its survival as the center of a network of colonies that were economically dependent upon enslaved-labor farming.

Tobacco cultivation, aside from being extremely labor intensive, had a pronounced tendency to deplete the soil, rendering it unproductive after two annual seasonal planting cycles. Consequently, new land had to be regularly cleared just to maintain a certain level of production. To increase production, enormous quantities of land and labor had to be accumulated. The enslavement farms could not be profitable using only Indigenous and indentured laborers or while limited to the land that they had already taken from the Powhatan. They needed increasingly more land and increasingly more laborers in order to produce enough tobacco to sell at a profit. So, they simply began stealing more Indigenous land, securing it for their exclusive use, and began importing kidnapped and trafficked African people as laborers.

The first African laborers were introduced into the English colonies in 1619. They were not, at this time, enslaved people. They were, under colonial law, classified as "indentured servants" bound to a certain "master" for a limited term of service. In that same year, twenty thousand pounds of tobacco were shipped to England, marking the beginning of a centuries-long epoch of institutionalized and racialized enslavement farming in North America, with African people targeted as the continent's most oppressed laboring class. Indentured labor contracts were routinely violated, resulting in extended periods of servitude. By the year 1630 there were more than a million and a half tons of tobacco being exported from the port at Jamestown each year, indicative of the increasingly long-term exploitation of African workers and the increased pressure being exerted against Indigenous communities for their lands.[1] By 1642, the first runaway labor laws were introduced to police the kidnapped African labor force.

By the end of the Powhatan wars of resistance in 1645, the Native population of the area had been reduced through disease and war by more than one half. By the end of the century, ninety percent of the original Powhatan society had been exterminated. Some survivors were integrated into various European settler colonies and enslaved, resulting in the loss of much of their cultural identity. Many others simply retreated into the swamps and moved as far away from the marauding European settlers as they could, forming scattered eco-communities along the many rivers and streams of the region. Doubtless, they were consciously seeking to maintain their social autonomy and ecological way of life.

THE ENSLAVED-LABOR FARMING SYSTEM

The vast swamps, bogs, and other similar landscapes were generally unfit for agriculturally dependent European settlement. Although real efforts were made, swamps were obstacles to most kinds of cash-crop cultivation and hostile to the development of products for the emerging global markets, with the possible exceptions of rice and sugar cane. But

1   Emily Jones Salmon and John Salmon, "Tobacco in Colonial Virginia,"
    in *Encyclopedia Virginia* (5 February 2021). https://encyclopediavirginia.org/
    entries/tobacco-in-colonial-virginia.

even these did not become suitable export monocrops from such a place as the Great Dismal Swamp.

Enslaved-labor rice farms sprang up just down the coast in what became the British colonies of South Carolina and later in Georgia. But large-scale sugar cane production was to find its home primarily in the lowland plains of the islands of the Caribbean and the lower reaches of the French-controlled Mississippi river delta. Up the coast and further inland along the plains of what became the colony of Virginia, a massive network of monocrop enslavement farms emerged, producing tobacco for export. What rice became to the development of the enslaved-labor system of colonial South Carolina and Georgia; tobacco had already become to the giant Virginia colony. While rice was confined within the swampy regions to the south, along the Carolina and Georgia coasts; tobacco was cultivated northward along the Virginia and the Chesapeake lowlands, but was blocked by the "great swampy" eco-systems of what would become the northeastern corner of the State of North Carolina. Over time, a network of tobacco-growing enslavement farms began to emerge, stretching much further inland along the moist flat lands of the coastal plains into the upcountry of both colonies. Tobacco proved to be the cash crop with greater longevity and protracted profitability for European colonizers.

BUILDING NEW ECO-COMMUNITIES
IN THE GREAT DISMAL SWAMP

By the beginning of the eighteenth century, the demographic landscape of southeastern Virginia and Northeastern North Carolina had dramatically changed. More than a century had passed since the first devastating contact with European colonizers. Toward the middle of the century, the enslaved population in eastern Virginia and the Chesapeake was well over one million people and was approaching fifty percent of the total colonial population.[2] The ecological impact of the widely spread network of tobacco-producing enslavement farms was clear and continuing.

An array of race-based enslavement-for-life laws were firmly in place by the first decade of the century as Indigenous lands were increasingly

---

2   Allan Kulikoof, *Tobacco and Slaves: The Development of Southern Cultures in the Chesapeake, 1680–1800*, (Chapel Hill: University of North Carolina Press, 1986), 332.

being colonized and the supply of European indentured labor was dwindling. The production of tobacco had become almost completely reliant upon African labor and stolen Native land for the immediate benefit of wealthy slave-owning white farmers. Moreover, an extensive network of buyers, transporters, investors, traders, and financial supporters were all now reliant upon the enslaved-labor farming system. In short, slavery had become a transatlantic industry that provided for an enormous amount of capital to be accumulated in the Americas, extracted from the backs of enslaved Africans laboring upon farmland stolen from Indigenous peoples.

A consistent and multi-racial pattern of resistance to this inhuman and anti-ecological onslaught had emerged from the earliest recorded attempts at European settlement. We must remember the seven hundred "cimarrons" of African heritage that Sir Frances Drake released at a location near Roanoke Island in 1586 and the "lost colony" of Europeans within this same general region.[3] Recall the winter of 1608–1609 in Jamestown, which is often remembered by U.S. historians as "the starving time." Many of the original English colonists joined a nearby Native community and never returned. Remember, too, the fragmentation of the Powhatan Confederacy as some of the smaller groups moved south and west into surrounding swamplands. But most of all, remember those runaway indentured laborers, formerly enslaved Africans, and Native people moving into the remote recesses of the Great Dismal Swamp who were creating actively resistant eco-communities— "maroon" communities— for nearly a century by the advent of the Tuscarora War" of 1711–1715.

From these early years of contact with Europeans it became clear that the Great Dismal Swamp was becoming a place of refuge for enslaved Africans, indentured Europeans, and any other people who sought freedom and a more ecological way of life. At any given time between the 1600s and 1850s, it is estimated that around two thousand people lived there, including a substantial population of Algonquian as well as Iroquois-speaking peoples.[4] Undoubtedly, there was some English and

---

3   For invaluable research on this racial dimension of the history of eastern North
      Carolina, see: Smallwood, "Tri-Racial Identity."
4   American University, "Freedom in the Swamp: Unearthing the secret
      history of the Great Dismal Swamp," *ScienceDaily*. www.sciencedaily.com/

Figure 6. Painting by Thomas Moran of African maroons in the Great Dismal Swamp, 1862.

Spanish spoken, and it is likely that some Arabic as well as other African languages became part of this creolized cultural mix. While creolization is usually regarded as an urban phenomenon, there nevertheless seems to have been a sufficient degree of sustained intra-swamp commercial and cultural intercourse for a creole culture to have developed over time within this remote rural area.[5]

It cannot be doubted that the inhabitants of the Great Dismal Swamp during this period were consciously running away from English colonial society, and later, the United States of America. In these necessarily remote places, runaways, fugitives, and freedom-seekers strived to create an autonomous existence and a directly democratic way of life that was more socially intimate and more symbiotically integrated with nature

releases/2011/05/110516075940.htm.
5   Smallwood, "Tri-Racial Identity."

as they lived their lives in direct defiance of encroaching capitalist violence and ecological destruction.

The Great Dismal Swamp was a regional magnet to the oppressed, the dispossessed, the defiant, the rebellious, and those who refused to be bound by the conventions of hierarchal society. Swamps were places where no horses or dogs could be used to hunt them down and where tobacco production simply could not take place. They were places of peace where loved ones could not be bought and sold. These were places where freedom seekers could build the intimately democratic communities where they could survive and thrive.

CHAPTER 4.
RESISTING THE SPREAD OF ENSLAVEMENT FARMING

As the avaricious land hungry enslaved-labor farm system pushed inland in Virginia and North Carolina, it came into deadly conflict with the Iroquois-speaking Tuscarora people. Tobacco farms could not spread directly south from Virginia into North Carolina because of the impediment of the Great Dismal Swamp around the Albemarle Sound. As we have already learned, swampland was hostile to tobacco production or any other form of large-scale for-profit agriculture of that era. By the very nature of its existence, the swamp exerted a definitive influence upon the social history of the region.

While the swamps offered refuge to the fugitives attempting to escape their exploitation and oppression to the east, the Tuscarora people offered it to them in inland regions. The Tuscarora had already been trading and attempting to make peace with the European settlers for almost a century. Over time, because of the geographical pattern of European settlement in North Carolina, they became divided into two distinctive bands: the Northern Tuscarora and the Southern Tuscarora.

The Northern band acquired metal tools and weapons in the lucrative fur trade and had become more Europeanized. They lived in the area of the Roanoke River to the west of the Albemarle Sound. Because of their large numbers and close commercial ties with the encroaching white settlements, they exerted a pronounced influence among other Native tribes who lived in the area.

The Southern Tuscarora, on the other hand, maintained more autonomy with respect to the growing populations of white settlers in and around the confluence of the Neuse and Trent rivers. This was a region where Southern Tuscarora had lived, farmed, and hunted for many years—a place where they were able to maintain a unified network of eco-communities with the town of Chattoka at its center. In 1710, the settler town of New Bern was established right next to Chattoka and large tracts of land were being appropriated by white settlers in the vicinity, in the face of increasing Indigenous indignation.

The Tuscarora—both Northern and Southern—had for years offered protection to fugitives and harbored runaways who escaped from enslavement farms throughout the region. Many of these refugees were, in the early years, Native people. Now they were mostly Africans. The European settlers, in turn, were stealing Tuscarora women and children, as well as African refugees under Tuscarora protection, enslaving or re-enslaving them upon capture. Both the Northern and Southern Tuscarora were being economically, racially, culturally, and politically transformed by virtue of their sustained contact with ever-increasing numbers of Europeans settlers in their midst, but it was the northern Tuscarora who were more greatly influenced.[1] In fact, it would be accurate to say that the Tuscarora of 1610 barely resembled the Tuscarora of 1710.

THE TUSCARORA WAR

Conflicts over enslavement and the direct confiscation of large tracts of Native lands were the root causes of the Tuscarora War. Hostilities broke out on 22 September 1711 as the Southern Tuscarora attacked settler enslavement farms scattered across a wide region, killing hundreds of farm owners and taking others as hostages. This proved to be a unique and defining characteristic of the conflict. Hostages were taken by the Tuscarora with the hope of exchanging them for members of their own communities who had been kidnapped and enslaved by the settlers.

An alliance of Native societies was formed, led by the Southern Tuscarora and composed of the Pamlico, the Cothechney, and Coree, Mattamuskeet and Machapunga, as well as African and mixed-race maroon communities. Together they mounted a bloody defensive war of

---

1   Arwin Smallwood, "Tri-Racial Identity of Tuscarora, Meherrin, Melungeon and Other Native Americans in North Carolina, Virginia and East to West."

resistance to drive out all Europeans from the central plains of North Carolina. The principal leader of the campaign was a man known as Chief Hancock. The Northern Tuscarora were neutral during this initial phase of the conflict. They were led by a colonial-appointed and culturally assimilated leader called Chief Tom Blount.[2]

The Tuscarora War was, in essence, one very bitter and bloody affair waged in two distinctive phases and lasted for nearly four years.[3] The first phase began with the 1711 assault by the Southern Tuscarora, which resulted in an overwhelming defeat of the North Carolina militia. As a result, the colony's governor requested reinforcements from the militias of both Virginia and of South Carolina.

Only the South Carolina government sent a well-armed force of thirty white militiamen and some five hundred Native mercenaries, mostly from the Yamasee, but also from the Wateree, the Congaree, the Waxhaw, and the Pee Dee. These forces, led by Colonel John Barnwell, arrived in January 1712 after a three-hundred-mile march. Some fifty local settlers joined them as they attacked the Tuscarora's Fort Neoheroka. The fort held, and a peace treaty was eventually signed there, signaling a cessation of hostilities and an end to the first phase of the war. The Tuscarora released their surviving hostages, but the colonial forces refused to do the same. They retained their prisoners in direct contravention of the treaty. Barnwell left with a number of captive Tuscarora, whom he sold into slavery in South Carolina.

The second phase of the war was distinguished by an unrelenting series of raids against the intrusive network of colonial enslavement farms. Again, North Carolina's colonial government was unable to respond to the increasing pressure brought against them by the Southern Tuscarora

---

2   The English names of these two Indigenous leaders indicate the degree of cultural assimilation that had taken place during the century of European colonization from 1609-1711.

3   This war was fought in Eastern North Carolina, beginning on 22 September 1711 to 11 February 1715. The belligerents on one side were: The colonial militias of Carolina (North and South) and Virginia, the Yamasee, the Apalachee, the Catawbas, the Cherokees, and later joined by the Northern Tuscarora. On the other side was the Southern Tuscarora, the Pamlico, the Cothechney, the Coree, the Neusiok, the Mattamuskeet and the Matchepungo.

and their allies. In a desperate move, the North Carolina governor promised Tom Blount of the Northern Tuscarora that he would appoint and recognize him as the "Chief" of all of the Tuscarora, both Northern and Southern, if the Northern Tuscarora would join the war on the side of the settlers. Shortly after his appointment, settlers began to refer to him as "Tom Blount, King of all Tuscarora." In a supreme act of deception and betrayal, forces led by "King Tom" captured Hancock and dutifully turned him over to the settler authorities, whereupon he was unceremoniously executed in 1712.

In December of that year, after the murder of Hancock, an even more massive militia force was dispatched from South Carolina on the request of the North Carolina governor. This time, colonial forces were commanded by Colonel James Moore Jr. The militia consisted of thirty-three colonial militia officers and almost one thousand well-armed Native mercenaries, including some of the same Native tribal groupings as the Barnwell-led force who had marched against the resisting Southern Tuscarora almost a year earlier.[4] The Yamasee again made up the vast majority of this army, but there were also significant additional contingents of the Apalachee, Catawba, and now the Cherokee. Most significantly, they also had the support of the Northern Tuscarora loyal to King Tom Blount.

The Southern Tuscarora had prepared several strong defensive positions by the time of the expected assault from the south, including Forts Torhunta, Innennits, and Catechna. The largest and most significant of the forts was the previously mentioned Neoheroka in North Carolina's present-day Greene County. All of these forts were destroyed in the war.

After many small skirmishes and pitched battles, the main body of the defiant Southern Tuscarora retreated back to Fort Neoheroka, where they made their final stand. On 1 March 1713 a three-week siege began. Even though the resisting Tuscarora had rifles and other small arms, along with their traditional weapons, the forces commanded by the South Carolina militia had large cannons and other explosives. Fort Neoheroka was incinerated during the battle. Hundreds of men, women, and children perished in the fire. Approximately 170 combatants were killed outside of

---

4   Jim Shamlin, "The Tuscarora War," *North Carolina Literary Review*, Vol. 1, No. 1
     (Summer, 1992).

the fort and some four hundred were kidnapped and trafficked to South Carolina, where they were sold into slavery.

With the defeat at Fort Neoheroka, remnants of the once-formidable Tuscarora were scattered. Most survivors were forced to migrate north into central Pennsylvania and into New York, where they became the sixth nation of the Haudenosaunee Confederacy. Others stayed in the region and fled into the swamps, where they were able to maintain a degree of social-ecological autonomy as they continued their resistance to colonial enslavement society up through the U.S. Civil War in the mid-nineteenth century. Some stayed with King Tom Blount and became part of his dwindling "kingdom," which at his death in 1731 was made up of a very small fraction of the Tuscarora left in the area that the settlers controlled through him. Many simply assimilated with other Indigenous communities, but never again became a force of unified resistance and defiance in their own name as Tuscarora people.

The betrayal of the Tuscarora by the corrupt authoritarian, "King Tom," represents a betrayal that was beyond the boundaries of the immediate conflict. It was a betrayal of the historic quest of an autonomous people for an intimate and directly democratic way of life. It was the betrayal of an entire culture.

The legacy of the Tuscarora survived not only as a component of the Haudenosaunee Confederacy and in the continued resistance to slavery emanating from the Great Dismal Swamp, but also in the multi-racial and multi-cultural makeup of eastern and central North Carolina's many rural communities, which persist to this day.[5] Many people in the region still self-identify as Tuscarora, even if they mostly identify with the places where they now live and continue to struggle.[6]

---

5   For a detailed account of the legacy of the Tuscarora along with the indentured European refugees and the African maroons who inhabited the Great Dismal Swamp, and who mounted a sustained campaign of resistance to enslavement from their eco-communities up to and including the Civil War, see: Neal Shirley and Saralee Stafford, *Dixie Be Damned: 300 Years of Insurrection in the American South* (Oakland: AK press, 2015).

6   Arwin Smallwood, "Tri-Racial Identity of Tuscarora, Meherrin, Melungeon and Other Native Americans in North Carolina, Virginia and East to West."

CHAPTER 5.
THE STRUGGLE MOVES SOUTH

The Yamasee were an amalgamation of Indigenous populations that emerged through a process of ethnogenesis just prior to the initial period of European influence on the southeastern Atlantic coast of what is now the State of Georgia. They spoke a Muscogean dialect and lived in a much more wide-spread network of villages and towns than did most other Indigenous societies of the time.

It is important to note that the process of larger Indigenous societies socially assimilating smaller ones involved the practice of relocating the women and children of smaller communities to the territory of a larger, more dominant group, as part of the resolution of a conflict. Historians often regard this practice as the taking of slaves. In reality, it was more akin to ritualized adoption. Women and their children became members of a cooperatively organized social formation with productive roles to be fulfilled by each member for the wellbeing of the collective. Their service, in such a situation, does not belong to a single individual. They are not owned by anyone. In that sense, they cannot be considered slaves. Women and children taken in after a conflict with other tribal groupings are expected, over a period of time, to assume the identity of the social formation into which they have been adopted. This practice is one of the ways that social expansion, cohesion, and greater sustainability was achieved. Ecological knowledge was also transferred and more widely diffused in this way. But when this practice became subverted and privatized for profit-making and labor-intensive production, it certainly becomes slavery in the violent form that is so familiar to us. This takes place when the social relations and collective social institutions are destroyed and laborers themselves are owned as the commodified property of individuals, families, or firms, and the services and products that are provided or produced by enslaved property belongs to the slaveowner.

This is precisely what was happening in the region of southeastern Georgia prior to contact with the Spanish invaders. The Yamasee were emerging as a homogeneous ethnic group by absorbing remnants of the once-large Guale society and other Native populations in the region. The Spanish had attempted to maintain a network of missions and had been engaged in the fur trade (deer skins were the principal commodity) and the trade in slaves among Native populations along the coast for almost a century by the time of the Yamasee War (1715-1717). The Spanish were engaged in the brutal destruction of all things Indigenous in their search for gold and silver. As a result of a brief and intense encounter involving some trade and social intercourse with the Spanish invaders, smaller Indigenous communities were decimated through infectious diseases and Spanish slave trading in Native people.[1] From this deadly conflagration with the Spanish, the Yamasee emerged as the largest remaining relatively homogenous Indigenous society in the region.

When it became clear to the Yamasee that the Spanish were spreading disease; were taking by force instead of fairly trading; and were seizing and selling members of their own tribe into enslavement; they revolted. Most of the Spanish missions on the coast and inland were burned or otherwise destroyed by the Yamasee. By 1675, the main body of their population moved north toward the Savannah River and into South Carolina. There they were able to assimilate other local groups within their social formation and increase their trade with the English colonial center of Charles Town.[2]

---

1 As the Spanish were not interested in settling and creating large agricultural enterprises in North America, early conflicts with them did not include conflicts over land as would later develop with the English.

2 The city of Savannah had not yet been founded, though there were some English trading posts along the side the Savannah river that would eventually become Georgia (the very last of the original 13 British colonies in North America) with the founding of the city of Savannah in 1733.

From around 1675 up to the outbreak of the 1711 Tuscarora War in North Carolina, the Yamasee followed a strategy of trade and collaboration with the growing English settler population in and around Charles Town. Over time, the once-lucrative fur trade began to decrease in importance as a major driver of commerce in the region. At the very same time, a rapid expansion of the enslavement farm system began to take hold. This oppressive and exploitative system was based upon the production of several cash crops, including rice, cotton, indigo, and sugar. Rice would soon emerge as the most profitable of these crops.

The settlers took advantage of the practice of the Yamasee and others to expand by the adoption of women and children and transformed this practice to involve the Yamasee in the colonial slave trade. Estimates vary for the numbers of Indigenous people enslaved and exported from the southeast and sold at slave markets from New England to Barbados from around twenty-four thousand to fifty-one thousand people between the years of 1670 and 1720. Regrettably, the Yamasee were very much involved in this human trafficking. With the revenue from the trade in Indigenous slaves, planters were able to buy skilled Africans who were familiar with rice cultivation, facilitating the rapid expansion of their rice production. From about 1708 to 1776, the enslaved African population in South Carolina ballooned to a level greater than the European population in the colony.[3]

The Yamasee were so well integrated into the life of the South Carolina colony that they had made up the largest proportion of the Native armed forces that were used to fight the Southern Tuscarora in North Carolina in the Tuscarora War (1711–1715). Immediately upon their return to South Carolina from that war, they had to respond to provocations that led to the Yamasee War (1715–1717) in the backcountry of South Carolina. Again, what has been called the Yamasee War was in fact a continuation of the Tuscarora War as both were part of a larger Indigenous war of resistance to European settlement of the Carolinas. The issues were the same and hostility was directed against the institutions of English settler colonialism and enslaved labor. They accused the

---

3   Joseph Hall, "The Great Indian Slave Caper", review of Alan Gallay, *The Indian Slave Trade: The Rise of the English Empire in the American South, 1670-1717* in *Commonplace*, Vol. 3, No. 1 (October 2002).

European settlers of being responsible for the decimation of their hunting grounds; the continued seizure of their lands; and the kidnaping of their women and children, many of whom were now of mixed raced or African descent; and defaulting on many of the agreements that they made. It was for these reasons that the Yamasee, along with an alliance of combined Native tribes with a large contingent of runaway self-emancipated maroons, mounted a campaign to drive the European settlers from the colony forever. Undoubtedly, the large number of self-emancipated maroons now living among the Yamasee helped to influence this change in attitude toward slavery.

This backcountry war involved the largest coalition of Natives and Africans that had ever been assembled in the history of anti-colonial and anti-slavery resistance in North America up until this point. The Yamasee themselves were an amalgamation of earlier Indigenous societies and represented the largest number of armed resistors. The Yamasee forces were supported by fighters from a broad coalition of Indigenous communities, including people from Muscogee, Cherokee, Catawba, Apalachee, Apalachicola, Yuchi, Shawnee, Congaree, Waxhaw, Pee Dee, Cape Fear, and Cheraw backgrounds, along with fighters from various African maroon communities and doubtlessly including those from the Great Dismal Swamp. A significant segment of almost all Indigenous societies and communities in South Carolina and Georgia took up arms against the expanding English aggression. As a result of the Tuscarora War, the Indigenous forces who had fought on the side of the South Carolina colony began to see that they had common cause with other Indigenous communities throughout the region. They also saw divisions among the colonialists. They formed an even wider and deeper alliance with African maroons and continued their war of resistance to settler-colonial aggression. They raided white settlements, killing the cheating river traders and hundreds of European settlers. Many of the settlers fled the upcountry regions and sought refuge in Charles Town, where people were literally starving. Before the fighting subsided in 1717, over seven percent of the South Carolina's total settler population was dead.[4] The conflict then

---

4   Steven J. Oatis, *A Colonial Complex: South Carolina's Frontiers in the Era of the Yamasee War, 1680–1730* (Lincoln: University of Nebraska Press, 2004), 167.

evolved into a protracted and bloody affair that lasted far beyond 1717, though most historians use this date to mark the official end of the war.

AFTERMATH OF THE YAMASEE WAR

The Yamasee's dramatic shift from allegiance to the English to an open war against them in only a matter of months is an indication of the uncertainty of colonial frontier life. The Cherokee and the Catawba left the Yamasee coalition in early 1716, which for many marked a turning point in the war. Loyalties changed in the wink of an eye and back again. These changes and reconfigurations of alliances occurred because of the resolution of old grievances and the emergence of new ones according to a collectively agreed upon system of justice and reciprocity among Indigenous populations.

However, a new dimension would become the principal determiner of alignment and realignment. Increasing commercial trade with English colonists began to be an important factor in the tentative and ever-shifting inter-communal Indigenous relations. Eventually, the Yamasee's rebel alliance and their African maroon allies were defeated and driven back across the Savannah River into Georgia. By this time, the Spanish presence along the eastern seaboard had grown substantially weaker in comparison to the English. This weakened position, paired with the gradual arrival of self-emancipated refugees who had escaped slavery in South Carolina, pushed Spanish colonialists to adopt a policy that encouraged African runaways to travel to the Spanish colonial city of St. Augustine and the eventual founding of Fort Mose, which we will discuss in Part Two of this volume.

Another often-overlooked consequence of the Yamasee wars was the actual founding of Savannah and the British colony of Georgia in 1733 as part of this struggle between conflicting Empires. The English had established a commercial outpost on the banks of the Savannah River, which had survived the hostilities of the war.[5] Originally settled as a yeoman

---

5   The trading post operated by John and Mary Musgrove had been commercially
    engaged with a group of economically dependent Yamasee (called "Yamacraw")
    people, led by a man named Tomochici. It was John (a white man) and
    Mary Musgrove, his wife (a Yamasee or Yamacraw), who met James Edward
    Oglethorpe (a white man from England) and his group on the bluff on the

farming province, the ownership of slaves was prohibited in the colony of Georgia from 1735 until 1751.

Despite the assertions of some historians, there were no enlightened humanitarian motivations at work behind this experimental policy. Georgia's elite colonial founders, including Governor General James Oglethorpe, were in no way opposed to the idea of enslaving African people for the benefit of white landowners. Georgia, however, was bordered by South Carolina to the north and Spanish Florida to the south and encompassed lands traversed by African refugees from South Carolina as they made their way to freedom in Spanish Florida. Establishing a white-only settler colony on this land is therefore more rightly understood as having the dual motivations of creating a buffer for the policing and recapturing of runaway Africans and establishing a garrison from which to defend South Carolina's lucrative enslavement farms from Spanish attack. Moreover, Oglethorpe and others feared that enslaved Africans living so close to Florida would doubtlessly escape to St. Augustine or otherwise aid the Spanish in undermining English colonial interests. The Georgia Experiment, as it is remembered today, did not last very long. In 1742, British forces—under the leadership of the absent Governor James Oglethorpe—won a military victory against a Spanish and African militia at the Battle of Bloody Marsh on St. Simons Island, after which Florida no longer represented a credible military threat to the English colonies. Over the next ten years, local white landowners pushed for a policy change and Georgia became an enslavement colony in 1751 as landowners began importing trafficked and enslaved African labor in an effort to develop large-scale rice agriculture.

That made it official. Among all thirteen colonies that would eventually break away from Britain to establish the United States of America, none prohibited the practice of human bondage and forced labor.

By the mid-eighteenth century, a number of important social and political changes were taking place across the southeastern region of North America: 1) the Yamasee were moving south to Florida through

---

south bank overlooking the Savannah River, where the city of Savannah stands today. This meeting has been designated as the occasion of the founding of Savannah and the colony of Georgia.

the buffer colony of Georgia, where they were becoming part of the larger amalgamated Muscogee-Creek Confederacy; 2) a massive surge in rice production along the coast of South Carolina, and later Georgia, was taking place; 3) rebellions of enslaved Africans were becoming more numerous, culminating in the Stono Rebellion of 1739 and indicating an increasing discontent among a rapidly expanding enslaved population; 3) more and more fugitives escaped slavery and were moving south into Spanish territory, driven by the promise of freedom and land; 4) a disciplined and self-organized "Black militia" made up of maroons who had fought in the Yamasee Wars were now regularly raiding rice plantations (enslavement farms) in South Carolina and Georgia from St. Augustine with the full authority of the Spanish Crown; and 5) the establishment of Gracia Real de Santa Teresa de Mose (known as Fort Mose) just north of St. Augustine in 1738.

In the midst of the confluence of all of this social motion and shifting demography in the early-mid eighteenth century, a most remarkable yet almost entirely unrecorded series of events was occurring: self-organized multi-racial eco-communities were being created throughout the Florida region, much as they had been in the Great Dismal Swamp. In these communities there lived African fugitives from rice-producing enslavement farms; Indigenous people of many distinctive cultural and linguistic backgrounds; and disgruntled, impoverished Europeans fleeing the rigid oppressive restraints of hierarchical society—they were freedom seekers all! These diverse self-governing villages, large and small, were called by many names, but mostly they were known by the river or stream on which they settled. They were often misunderstood as if they were solely Indigenous communities, but they were multi-racial and diverse, both ethnically and linguistically.

These diverse eco-communities varied in size, as they moved and grew over time. Some were clustered in the vicinity of St. Augustine. Many others were scattered throughout the backwoods and swamps of northern Florida. They maintained complex and often contentious relationships with the Spanish and English colonial governments that claimed conflicting regional jurisdictions. Throughout the next century, they were a dynamic and ever-present aspect of Florida's evolving social ecology as they maintained their resilient autonomy. Later, such communities of "cimarrons" became known as the "Seminole Indians," having been given this designation for purposes of ethnic cleansing in the early and middle nineteenth century as part of the Indian Removal Acts, implemented by the racist U.S. government.

From 1790 to 1810, those maroons who remained at the Great Dismal Swamp participated in a continuous chain of resistance actions against the enslavement farm system, including armed guerrilla assaults on the farms and their overseers. It has even been suggested that Great Dismal Swamp maroons may have helped to coordinate nearly every rebellion, conspiracy, and insurrection of enslaved people in the region surrounding the swamp during this period.[6]

Historians often place the end date of wars at a decisive battle or a peace treaty which allowed for the occupation of the territory of one side of the conflict by the forces of the other. That might be sufficient in some cases, but the wars of Indigenous and maroon resistance did not end with a decisive battle because the ongoing skirmishes were associated with a larger-scale conflict that has by now continued for centuries. This war could never end with a treaty, because such treaties have never been honored by colonizing governments. They existed only to contain the resistance of Indigenous peoples and maroons while allowing invasion, oppression, and genocide to continue unabated. Through it all, the struggle continues and has taken many distinctive forms. Its essence, though evolving, remains fundamental to the social-ecological future of this region, to the planet, and to all of its living beings.

For now, let us turn our attention south as our story continues in Spanish Florida.

---

6   Neal Shirley and Saralee Stafford, *Dixie Be Damned*, 42.

Part Two: Fort Mose

CHAPTER 6.
THE HUMAN IMPULSE FOR FREEDOM

Within the limited descriptive literature about Gracia Real de Santa Terea de Mose (hereafter referred to as Fort Mose), this autonomous community of self-emancipated Africans living in Spanish Florida from 1738 until 1763 is inaccurately portrayed, over the short and distinctive times of its existence, as responding to the whims of the various competing colonial efforts of European nation states as they sought to establish a settler presence in the Americas. This presence is dominantly accepted as the standard of human social progress within the "New World."

The strong and manifest impulse of the Africans of Fort Mose toward an independent, self-directed, developmental trajectory is seldom comprehended with all of its critical implications. Enslaved Africans' intense quest for freedom and autonomy, rooted in their rich history from the Guinea Coast, has never been fully incorporated into any analysis of this community. This, of course, short-circuits any meaningful comprehension of the internal dynamics of the collective self-governance of the African inhabitants of Fort Mose or any other maroon community in the Americas during that period. This chapter will show that the previous collective experience of Africans prior to enslavement—and not an attempt to imitate various European colonial societies—motivated the freedom seekers of Fort Mose.

Our goal, more broadly, is to reverse one of the greatest misconceptions in the historiography of social movements. Almost without a hint of exception, human history has been told from the perspective of various authoritative individual personalities and their roles within the administrative apparatuses of various hierarchical social formations as they came and went throughout recorded history. Consequently, little or no attention has been paid to the much smaller in scale, less hierarchal, more social egalitarian, more *intimate*, social-ecological formations that existed on the periphery of larger and more centralized societies. Often these peripheral social formations, on the edge of what is arrogantly considered "civilization," have been condemned as "primitive," "savage," "barbarian," "infidel," "hordes," and assumed to be comparatively less advanced or less developed. This prejudicial notion is based upon a wooden materialist analysis of a given society such that a society which has the greater capacity to produce goods on a larger scale is regarded as more "developed" or more "advanced" than others of lesser material capacity—even when these goods have no use and contribute nothing to the collective enhancement of the society that is responsible for their production and distribution and often result in waste and ecological degradation. This dangerously inhuman line of reasoning has become the moral compass that justifies all manner of death, destruction, and carnage as somehow necessary in order for human society to continue to make progress.

Most of our surviving written histories are derived directly from narratives sponsored by the ruling classes of these materially-driven societies; they conceive the production, distribution, and consumption of material wealth as the most significant human social endeavor—a pervasive worldview throughout human societies in the twenty-first century. In one way or another, most historians today interpret the entire trajectory of human social progress in this narrow and obtuse fashion. This dominant conceptualization of history serves to benefit and reinforce the interests of those who rule above society today, via multi-national corporations and various coalitions of nation-states, at the expense of everyone else.

Fort Mose, on the other hand, was a very small and short-lived frontier social formation of very limited material means. But when considered as an example of community self-organization, in which oppressed people had created a society where their human social potential could be realized to a greater extent than the colonial enslavement which they had summarily rejected and escaped, this small collective should be understood as very "advanced" and "developed" indeed. Small though it was, Fort Mose had great human social significance. We will return to this when we advance some specific arguments regarding the internal governance of this community. Additionally, the conscious social and ecological development of the Indigenous peoples of the region has never been considered in relation to the development of Fort Mose or any of the other maroon communities that came into being as a result of this titanic and protracted clash of political, economic, and cultural systems at this historical conjuncture. In the pages that follow, you are invited to examine Fort Mose as a site of convergence—only one example of many—between these respective African and Indigenous North American traditions of intimate direct democracy.

THE SOCIAL ECOLOGY OF INDIGENOUS SOCIETIES

Fort Mose came into being after almost 230 years of violent colonization and genocidal destruction, waged against a vast network of Indigenous communities and cultures in the Americas. In the early 1500s, Portuguese, Spanish, English, French, and Dutch settler colonialists established sustained contact with a large network of Indigenous agricultural communities in the Americas that were developing a remarkably unique pattern of regional interconnectivity as they exchanged goods and ideas. Within what is now the southeastern United States, from the Atlantic coast in the east to the Mississippi River in the west, and to the Gulf of Mexico in the South, a variety of distinctive linguistic and cultural communities could be seen.[1] This network of communities eventually became part of a contested peripheral zone of competing European empires. Aside from the superficial glorification of European "explorers," however, mainstream historians have generally neglected to study these regions, and the social and ecological knowledge that was being generated there prior to contact with Europeans. Nor have they thoroughly considered many of the negative consequences of the fateful contact itself.

These eco-communities, almost without exception, were communal societies with limited social hierarchy and where nature was, by and large, not seen as a resource to be exploited by humanity. Almost all basic human needs were provided for by a direct and sustainable reciprocity with the

---

1   Roxanne Dunbar-Ortiz, *An Indigenous Peoples' History of the United States* (Boston: Beacon Press, 2014), 23–25.

immediate environment. While certain specific skills might vary among individuals or regions, knowledge of significant manual technology was held in common and products that were derived from the application of these technologies were distributed along some equable principle and used directly by members of the community. While there was some limited and expanding production of goods for exchange, primary production remained for direct and immediate use. The exchange of goods with more or less equal value were traded with other communities and possessed some utility for both the producers and the users where the production and the trade took place in different communities. Remarkably, these exchanges were usually not even considered to be "trade" in the market-oriented or capitalistic sense of the term, but were instead understood as the presentation of gifts. Such exchanges were one of the many ways that these eco-communities were interconnected as social relationships expanded to accept "others" outside of the narrow confines of kinship-based clans and form larger communities. Even so, the notion that a single individual might exclusively "own" resources, tools, or knowledge which the community required for its collective livelihood and its reciprocal interaction with the rest of the natural world was simply unknown.[2]

Simply put, Indigenous worldviews pertaining to humanity's relationship to nature, at both the individual and communal levels, were far different from those of the conquering Europeans. The slow, deliberate, intimate, and sustained rhythm of village life, with daily face-to-face social interaction and complex individual and communal responsibilities, fashioned a pervasive conception of their collective social existence. Broadly speaking, this was the manner in which Indigenous societies of the region were self-governed, ecologically evolving, and defining the ways in which each and every individual in the community could conceptualize and realize their better selves. It was an understanding of the self that was rooted in and grew from the community from which they were born and with which they maintained a dynamic social interconnectivity throughout their lives. Of course, these Native communities varied widely in their political and social diversity. They ranged from the massive, centralized,

---

2   Sebastian Junger, *Tribe: On Homecoming and Belonging* (New York: Twelve Press, 2016), 14–15.

and hierarchical urban cultures of the Aztecs, Maya, the Incas—and for our purposes, the lesser-known Cahokia—to the smaller, less complex, more autonomous communal and equalitarian cultures scattered throughout what is now the whole of North, South, and Central America as well as within the Caribbean archipelago.

PRE-CONTACT INDIGENOUS CONFEDERATIONS

The Indigenous communities on the perimeter of the Gulf of Mexico and the islands of the Caribbean basin can be shown to have been an integral part of a wide-ranging cultural exchange. It is therefore a mistake to assume, as some have, that the Gulf of Mexico and the Caribbean Sea were barriers to social integration. On the contrary, given the naval technologies of the time, these large bodies of water and their auxiliary waterways were a means of connecting peoples and cultures over vast distances. These Indigenous communities were thriving in the pre-Colombian era, but the coming of murderous Conquistadors, and later the avaricious profit-seeking European settlers, proved to be more than they could withstand. Among the earliest victims of European invasion were the Caribs, Arawak, Taino, and Chibchan-speaking peoples of the islands of the Caribbean. These communities were mercilessly attacked and nearly eradicated, but remarkably survived as they integrated with self-liberated communities of formerly enslaved African maroons, like the present-day Garifuna of central America.[3]

The general developmental dynamic of interrelated Native communities prior to significant European settler contact can be seen in the dynamic evolution of two relatively independent networks of Indigenous societies. The first ranged from the Great Lakes to the St. Lawrence River and the Atlantic Ocean, extending south through what is now Pennsylvania, Virginia, and eastern North Carolina. This was a massive, diverse, interrelated network of sometimes scattered and sometimes clustered villages numbering into the tens of thousands. Historians sometimes refer to this configuration of six discernable clusters of extended kinship and common linguistic groupings as the "Iroquois Confederation," but it is more accurately remembered as the Haudenosaunee Confederacy and was

---

3   Dunbar-Ortiz, *An Indigenous Peoples' History of the United States*, 23–24.

comprised of the Seneca, the Cayuga, the Onondaga, the Oneida, the Mohawk, and later the Tuscarora peoples.[4] This confederation emerged as a large defensive network of linked communities based upon an expanded identity derived from a complex and interdependent pattern of production and trade. The Tuscarora belonged to the southeastern most reaches of this Indigenous confederation and inhabited what is now southeastern Virginia and east-central North Carolina. Many anthropologists place the Cherokee, who at that time inhabited the mountainous region known today as North Carolina, northern Georgia, and eastern Tennessee, among this group because their language is a subdivision of the "Iroquoian" language family.[5] Even though their language was distinctive, it belonged to the same basic linguistic group of the Haudenosaunee and there is evidence that the Cherokee are culturally related to Native peoples from the Great Lakes region. As we discussed in Part One, the relationship of the Cherokee to the Haudenosaunee Confederacy is particularly important to our study of the Great Dismal Swamp and our understanding of Indigenous interaction with European settler colonialism in the northeastern part of the continent.

The second Indigenous confederation, the Muscogee-Creek Confederacy, is germane to our understanding of European settlement in the southeastern region of the United States and the emergence of Fort Mose. This federation was made up of the Muscogee, the Chickasaw, the Choctaw, and the Natchez peoples toward the west in the Mississippi Valley. This evolving confederation eventually came to include the Seminoles in Spanish Florida at a subsequent historical period. The latter represented a special case, and with this exception, the above are regarded as the major distinctive Native ethnic communities of the southeastern region of North America when significant European influence began to

---

4   Dunbar-Ortiz, *An Indigenous Peoples' History of the United States*, 25.

5   The present author hesitates to use the concept of "nation" in this context, preferring to use it in reference to the European centralized nation-states of the capitalist period. The terms of choice in connection with the Native Americans grouping of this period are: ethnic groupings, clans, communities, cultures, societies, or civilizations. The term "tribes" is definitely not preferred because of the racist implications of the term.

be felt.[6] Both of these huge federations were undergoing continuous integration of smaller local clans as they evolved. This dynamic natural social process of configuration and reconfiguration as they developed, grew, and followed their unique path toward the realization of their human social potential in symbiosis with nature was reflective of who these people were and who they were becoming. But at the point in their development the initial European conquest began, they comprised small and intermediately sized villages and the whole federation was governed by a relatively flat political structure. That is, there was no nobility to speak of, and therefore, a social conflict based upon distinctive internal social classes was either limited or non-existent.

The Muscogee-Creek are known to be related to the great "Mississippian Mound Builders" of the southeastern woodlands, whose culture pre-dates European contact by as much as a thousand years or more. By the tenth century, a single centralized massive city state had emerged in what is the present-day mid-Mississippi River Valley near what is now the city of St. Louis on the opposite bank of the Mississippi River.[7]

CAHOKIA AND THE DEVELOPMENT OF THE SOUTHEASTERN NATIVE COMMUNITIES

The center of this vast and influential culture was Cahokia, a city distinguished by pyramid-shaped earthen mounds of various sizes that spread throughout an urban area that supported a population numbering approximately 20,000 around the year 1050 CE.[8] Like many other

---

6   Prior to the initial contact with European settlers there were no "Seminoles." The Seminoles emerged in response to hostile European settlement and their population included a substantial number of self-emancipated Africans and ethnically mixed communities of Native, African, and even European people.

7   James M. Collins, *The Archaeology of the Cahokia Mounds* (Springfield: Preservation Agency, 1990). For a comprehensive exposition of the Archeological exploration of the site see: Warren K. Moorehead, Edited by John E. Kelly, *The Cahokia Mounds* (Tuscaloosa: University of Alabama Press, 2000).

8   Dunbar-Ortiz, *An Indigenous Peoples' History of the United States*, 23. Cahokia is estimated to have been larger than London during the same period.

Figure 7. An artistic reconstruction of twelveth-century Cahokia by Lloyd Townsend, exhibited as a mural at the Cahokia Mounds Museum and Interpretive Center.

cities around the world, it was home to an ethnically and linguistically diverse population. Recent evidence shows that this huge commercial and cultural center was largely inhabited by people who came from other places—perhaps from as far away as the Great Lakes to the north or the Gulf Coast to the south.[9] By the fourteenth century, however, the city was all but abandoned. The reason for Cahokia's abandonment is today considered a mystery of North American archeology.

Many anthropologists believe that a single event caused this precipitous decline—perhaps a flood or an earthquake. This, however, is a misconception born out of historian's common emphasis on the study of large centralized societies at the expense of any serious examination of the more decentralized, smaller-scale societies that emerge on the edges of these dominions. This same dominant historiographic approach seeks only to record the stories of hereditary monarchs, kings, emperors, tsars, maharajas, pharaohs, or any sort of potentates or sovereign within a specific regional domain, kingdom, fiefdom, or space organized under a ruling elite. The democratic desires and capacities for self-organization among the tens of thousands of ordinary people living in a place like Cahokia are simply not considered.

---

9   Megan Gannon, "The First US City Was Full of Immigrants," *Live Science*, 6 March 2014. https://www.livescience.com/43896-cahokia-ancient-city-immigrants.html

Viewed from another perspective, however, we can see that this decline could just as easily have taken place because of some conscious rebellion stemming from internal social conflict. Such conflict could have certainly existed in combination with natural disasters or ecological catastrophe, resulting in increased instability in the social relations from within.

We have seen, for example, tightly knitted hereditary monarchies, in which institutional authority rests in the hands of a small ruling minority, become highly unstable within a few generations. Such societies also typically demonstrate extractive economic relationships with nature and have historically been unable to maintain their integrity in the face of various natural crises. Often the internal social organization of hierarchical societies contributes to the intensification of these types of natural crises. And of course, when a natural crisis occurs it is the most oppressed classes of society that suffers the greatest loss and experiences a disproportionate share of the pain. Cahokia, in the years just before its demise, was organized and ruled in just such a fashion and so was vulnerable to just this type of social disintegration.

Cahokia had developed a rigid class structure with a small, hereditarily-determined elite caste or class who did not labor and who exerted substantial control over a lucrative regional trading center. This class also organized labor on its own terms, which generated a substantial accumulated material surplus and, as a result, an oppressed population of laborers was created at the bottom of the society. In fact, Cahokia, from all indications, was the embodiment of a genuine state held together by extreme forms of coercion. As such, Cahokia, like all hierarchical social formations, was greatly susceptible to both the periodic and naturally occurring disasters external to the society and the human social crisis arising from within the contradictory layers and institutions of the society itself.

As Cahokia's centralized state power destabilized over time, a new competing world view began to take shape. In fact, we could argue that the decline of Cahokia was conscious and that many of the society's underclasses began to develop their own less oppressive and more autonomous communities away from and beyond the reach of the centralized authority of any dominant clan or state.[10] In the wake of Cahokia's prolonged

---

10   Jane Mt. Pleasant, a scholar of Tuscarora descent and professor emeritus of agricultural science at Cornell University, has similarly argued that the

decline there emerged a profusion of numerous, widely scattered villages throughout the Southeastern region with similar languages and mound-building practices, as well as other cultural similarities to that of Cahokia. The archeological remains of these communities can be seen all over the central and southeastern region of the contemporary U.S. along the shifting banks of many rivers and creeks.[11]

Interestingly, there were no hereditary rulers to be found within any of the Muscogee villages and towns that emerged in the region where Cahokia once governed as a state power. Could it be that the decline of Cahokia, in fact, represents the rise of less hierarchical, more intimate, directly democratic ecological societies? These communities may have looked and sounded architecturally and linguistically like Cahokia, but they did not smell politically or socially like Cahokia at all. Their worldview, as derived from their social life, was quite different. Their understanding of group existence was more intimately integrated with the rest of the natural world, of which they saw themselves as a distinctive part.

As they attempted to escape the crippling oppression of a large inhuman hierarchical state, these federated social splinters from the remains of the once-centralized Cahokian culture grew into what eventually became known as the Muscogee-Creek Confederacy. While there was some limited hierarchy in Muscogee villages and towns, there was nothing like the rigid class/caste state structure of Cahokia. Prior to European invasion, these villages, towns, and the larger federation itself were all essentially governed by a form of structured consensus decision-making, with the most influential members of the community typically exerting the most persuasive credibility. This was a binding but reviewable consensus reached in a face-to-face discussion based upon an intimate knowledge of each person's potential for service to the continued sustainability and prosperity of the society. Muscogean peoples created dynamic institutional relations with defined roles that conveyed and communicated their collectively acquired knowledge. In these ways, and many others, their

---

abandonment of the Cahokia site was a political and cultural shift towards decentralization and away from state power. See Asher Elbein, "What Doomed a Sprawling City Near St. Louis 1,000 Years Ago?", *The New York Times*, 24 April 2021.

11   A small fraction of these sites have been preserved as National and State Parks.

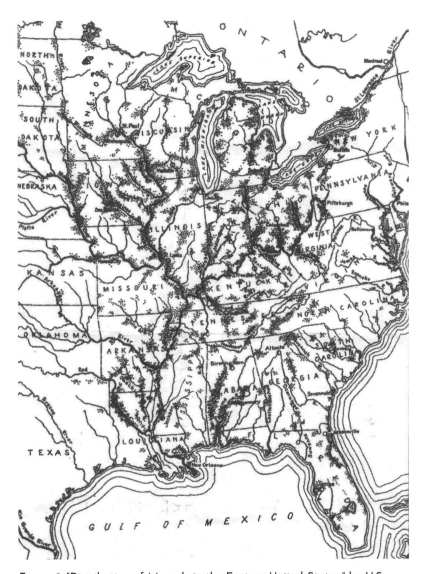

Figure 8. "Distribution of Mounds in the Eastern United States," by U.S. ethnographer and archeologist Cyrus Thomas, 1894. Note that each dot represents an entire mound site, not individual mounds. Courteousy of the Ocmulgee Mounds National Historical Park.

political and social life was far more democratic than that of the conquering Europeans.

THE INTIMATE SELF-ORGANIZATION OF THE MUSCOGEE CREEK VILLAGE

Upon close examination of these relatively autonomous towns and their internal governance, we find the institutional role of the Mico. Popularly misrepresented by historians as a village chief or autocratic headman, this male member of the community was, in reality, socially influential because of his knowledge of the natural world. This has often been simplistically interpreted as his having been a skilled hunter. He is probably physically strong and athletic enough to be an effective hunter and an otherwise effective gather of food, but he is also a teacher, and therefore a sharer of accumulated knowledge from which the whole community could benefit. He was also a convincing debater within the assembled council or lodge. Decisions of the council or lodge were also binding upon the Mico as a proto-executive. Micos have often been mistaken by uncritical scholars as having been analogous to nobility or royalty, but this position was not inherited. Micos did not rule as authoritarian figures but were respected as guides in the making of collective decisions. It was the council that ruled. The Mico, however, did steer the discussion as he presided within the council.[12]

Micos were assisted in governance by Henihas. They were usually younger and less experienced but many of them acquired great prestige

---

12 David Graeber and David Wengrow likewise present a directly democratic perspective on the Indigenous societies of southeastern North America and the evolving role of the Mico in *The Dawn of Everything: A New History of Humanity* (New York: Farrar, Straus and Giroux, 2021) 471–473.

It is also worth noting that *The Dawn of Everything* is the last book by David Graeber and was published posthumously after his death in September 2020. Graeber was an anarchist activist and prominent anthropologist who is perhaps best remembered for his public involvement with the Occupy Wall Street movement in 2011. While his activism often placed him at odds with academic employers, his work will be long remembered for challenging many dominant misconceptions about human history and championing humanity's directly democratic impulses. (M.K and A.Z.)

and influence within the council. This occurred as a result of consistent dedication and civic service or some extraordinary deed or demonstrated knowledge that the community as a whole could benefit from. Henihas often became Micos as their influence grew and the previous Mico became less effective because of age or for some other reason. Among some of the other evolved functionary roles was a Tustunnuggee, a person (usually a male) with great physical strength that was a ranking warrior who possess certain fighting knowledge and skills. His role was to make sure that the security of the community was organized and protected from external threat.

Since Muscogee Creek social formations of this period were uniformly matrilineal, women, most especially elderly women, played a distinctive role. They nurtured the young; they cultivated, gathered, and prepared food; they arranged marriages, and made decisions about the intro-domestic space. They also played a decisive role in the designation and accountability of the Mico, a role that was informed by their intimate knowledge of each community member's character and personality from childhood to adulthood. Then there was the most enigmatic and complex figure in this early Native American community, the Yahola, whom scholars have sometimes reductively designated a "witch doctor" or shaman.[13] The Yahola served as a cultural teacher and guide in the preservation of the traditions that provided historical continuity and shared collective identity of the village and the larger federation. Yaholas usually possessed an intricate and detailed knowledge of medicinal plants, which the villagers used for the treatment of sicknesses and injuries. They did not, however, monopolize this knowledge, even if they sometimes attempted to do just that. Yaholas also presided at ceremonies that were occasions for the teaching and learning of the community's traditions and folkways. Often, they embellished myths and lore in order to increase their prestige and legitimacy within the community. This was often the source of much intrigue as their verbal recall and exaggerated recollections were often called into question, since there was no written record of events. They

---

13   Andrew Frank, "Creek Indian Leaders." *New Georgia Encyclopedia*, 25 August 2020. https://www.georgiaencyclopedia.org/articles/history-archaeology/creek-indian-leaders.

were usually among the oldest members of the community and, as such, were assumed to have greater wisdom and practical knowledge. This was often not the case and they frequently relied on deception in order to gain and maintain influence within the village.[14]

These changing communities remained reliant upon a somewhat similar set of assigned roles. It is clear that, prior to the establishment of European settler-colonies, these cultures and those with whom they symbiotically engaged, and even those that they absorbed, were fundamentally non-hierarchical and relatively flat in their social organization. Gender, age, and clan differences were recognized and organized for mutual benefit. They were devoid, however, of a centralized state and contained no crystalized classes or castes to any significant degree.

This federation of extended clans, villages, and towns of Indigenous people in the southeastern region of North America, following this general yet unique pattern of dynamic self-organization, is of great importance to our study of Fort Mose.[15] These relatively autonomous and democratic eco-communities of various sizes, profusely scattered along the rivers and creeks of the region, were the first to encounter European colonists, and both enslaved and free Africans, in the seventeenth century.[16]

While it is generally acknowledged that there is a tendency for communal societies to become more socially stratified over time, it is also accepted—particularly among Marxist social theorists—that these stratified social formations tend to develop into large centralized states if they continue to make "progress." Historians then study these large, centrally

---

14   For a more complete explanation of the emergence of role of the Shamans from that of the Yaholas as the elders asserted their dominance in pre-class communities, see: Murray Bookchin, *The Ecology of Freedom*, 152–158.

15   Peter Nabokov, *Native American Testimony: A Chronicle of Indian-white Relations from Prophecy to the Present, 1492-2000* (New York: Penguin, 1991), 4–5.

16   English-speaking settlers simply designed any Native community that they found living on the banks of a river or creek as "creek Indians." This was and remains the source of much confusion. This gross designation included many non-Muscogee and failed to identify the Muscogee as a larger unified society. This is only one consequence of the broader historical problem of white settlers have using inaccurate, ahistorical, and racist categories for the development and implementation of racist governmental policies as the settler colonies grew into fully fledged white-supremacist nation-states.

governed formations as high points in "civilization." This perspective is, at least, questionable.

Who is to say that Indigenous peoples could not have pursued a different, less ecologically damaging, development if left alone?[17] Who is to say that they were not doing just that when they came under the withering social firestorm that was visited upon them by colonization and commercial capitalism, with its private property, insatiable markets, wasteful production, and the private ownership and sale of everything on such a massive scale? As we critically consider the early contact of enslaved and free Africans under the domination of Portuguese, Spanish, English, Dutch, and French colonialists with Indigenous peoples, we must realize that the inhuman and immoral right to conquest and domination that European capitalists have asserted for five hundred years is at least unjust, and at most, has brought the Earth to the brink of planet-wide ecological catastrophe.

THE GENOCIDAL WAR AGAINST INDIGENOUS NORTH AMERICANS

When the Europeans arrived, southeastern North America was lined with connecting trails, navigable rivers, and flowing streams that were part of an evolving transportation infrastructure indicating a substantial degree of sustained social intercourse and complex cross-cultural interaction within and between a multitude of diverse yet integrated human societies. This region had a greater abundance of rivers, streams, lush vegetation, game animals, and rich fertile soil than most other regions of the Europeans' known world. The seasons were moderate, full of sunshine and atmospheric moisture. Most of all, the people here were organically integrated in a dynamic symbiosis with each other and the natural world.[18] The European newcomers, by and large, did not seek to understand Indigenous worldviews or lifestyles. They simply condemned

---

17   Bookchin, *The Ecology of Freedom*, 158.

18   Dynamic and symbiotic relationships are relationships that are free of
conflict, perhaps even violent and deadly conflict. What is to be stressed here
is that these societies were forging evolving and interconnective communal
networks that were being systematically ripped asunder by the European settler
occupation, expansion, and protracted genocidal warfare.

them as primitive, backward, and barbaric. To the settler-colonialist eye, Indigenous life lacked dynamism and would forever remain unchanged and static.

Perhaps Europeans were blind to the form and nature of Indigenous North American social-ecological interaction because of the exploitative social organization that dominated the very societies from which these conquering thieves came. Emerging European empires and nation states had developed sharply conflicting social classes with coercive domination already fully established at their cores. Moreover, it could be argued that European societies had developed a truly adversarial relationship to nature. Europeans viewed nature as a material resource created by an absolutist god and put on earth only for the exploitation, blind greed, and self-righteous glory of those who ruled.[19] As a result of European conquest and the violent imposition of this worldview, Indigenous communes and federations, and their social-ecological knowledge, have never been fully appreciated or respected by mainstream historians, especially those working in the European academic tradition.

There are many explanations concerning the causes of the five-hundred-year genocide suffered by Indigenous peoples in North America. Some say that it was the introduction of diseases to which Native people's immune systems could not adjust that ultimately caused unchecked serious illness and widespread deaths. Others argue that it was an alien social system that inflicted most of the damage. Doubtless, there were many deaths caused by disease. Certainly, there was great social and economic dislocation and damage. In the final analysis, however, it was and is a protracted war of attrition, conquest, and genocidal mass-murder in the most vicious, brutal, and militaristic sense—a conflict punctuated by some of the cruelest massacres of innocent people that the world has ever witnessed.

In this continuing genocide, not only have countless numbers of human lives been lost, but the enormous and simultaneous displacement of Indigenous knowledge about ecological and social systems is only now

---

19   The development of this mechanical, exploitable view of nature is discussed in depth in Carolyn Merchant, *The Death of Nature: Women, Ecology, and the Scientific Revolution* (New York: HarperCollins, 1989).

being comprehended. All of this violence was being done in the name of "progress." Of course, this could be considered progress from the perspective of ascendant European commercial classes bent upon accumulating wealth at all costs; but historians must ask ourselves whether this was "progress" from the point of view of those Indigenous peoples whose communities were (and still are) being destroyed, or from the perspective of trafficked and enslaved African people, or, to a lesser extent, the European laborers who were also exploited. Ethical, critically-minded historians must affirm and clarify that colonialism and genocide are evils that can never be regarded as any part of human social progress and can never be justified in history.

CHAPTER 7.
THE PEOPLES OF AFRICA'S GUINEA COAST

The Trans-Atlantic trade in enslaved labor (sometimes referred to as the "triangular" slave trade) involved the entire African continent and all of its peoples, in societies large and small, from the early 1500s through the middle 1800s. This protracted process, taking place along the entire western coast of Africa, involved the forcible mass-transfer of human labor and skill on a scale never before seen in human history. During this period, this coastline was popularly referred to as the Guinea Coast.

Prior to the beginning of this infamous human trafficking, the Guinea Coast received successive waves of people migrating from the interior.[1] The relatively large, centralized, and socially hierarchical states of the Western Sudan—Ghana in the ninth through eleventh centuries; Mali, whose heyday spanned the thirteenth and fourteenth centuries; and Songhai, which maintained regional hegemony from the fifteenth through the sixteenth centuries—can be said to be responsible for the general exodus of diverse ethnic communities moving toward the coast.[2] The latest of these arrivals was the massive population known as the Mende who, like other groups arriving in the area, were part of the generalized response to the social conflicts within and among these states. This migration is reminiscent of the movement and cultural diffusion of the Muscogee-Creek in North America along the rivers of the southeastern region of North

---

1   Walter Rodney, *A History of the Upper Guinea Coast, 1545 to 1800*, (Oxford University Press, 1970), 10.
2   Walter Rodney, *How Europe Underdeveloped Africa*, (London: Bogle-L'Ouverture Publications, 1972), 66–72.

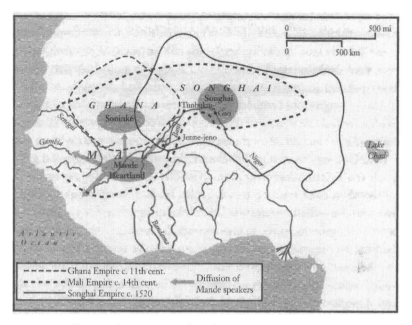

Figure 9. Diffusion of Mande speakers from source areas of empire formation in the Western Sahel, eight to sixteenth centuries. Note the migration of peoples toward the coast and away from centers of state power, especially those arriving outside of the boundary of Mali Empire in the fourteenth century. Source: Jane Landers, *Black Rice*, Figure 2.2.

America, which happened to be occurring during the same time some eight thousand miles away. While the migration of the Muscogee Creek seems to have occurred in one continuous wave away from a single state, Cahokia, the migration of peoples toward the coast in the Western Sudan took place in multiple overlapping waves fleeing a number of centrally organized states over time.

The Guinea Coast was settled by a network of Indigenous communities prior to the arrival of the Portuguese in the fifteenth century. These communities were much more numerous and concentrated than those of the Muscogee peoples in North America. The villages of the Guinea Coast tended to be larger in size, some with as many as two or three thousand inhabitants. The existence of larger cities was the exception to the rule in such a vast region. These intricately interrelated communities were the smaller-scale remains of the more massive centralized states of the Western Sudan. As such, they bore the indelible cultural and economic mark of their previous existence as peripheral frontier societies spreading west from the large, but declining, interior kingdoms. Even so, these federated clusters of thousands of villages were essentially stateless societies.[3]

As successive waves of migrants from the large interior states arrived at various points along the coast, they gradually assimilated existing villages along the banks of the vast network of rivers that led to the Atlantic Ocean. This process resulted in a profusion of ethnic groupings with distinctive languages and customs, owing to the complex configuration of events that unified them, the circumstances that drove their initial migration, and the cultures of those people with whom they came into contact as they contributed to the evolving societies of the coastal region over time.

Population growth along the coast was, in part, a reflection of the greater quantities and varieties of goods available within large regional markets. These were primarily agricultural societies. That is to say, they grew their own food. There were farmers that grew yams using iron tools. Others produced large quantities of millet.[4] Some communities also had significant numbers of cattle and goats. But it was the rice farmers using refined irrigation technology and sophisticated methods in the production of "wet rice" that is most significant to the ecological narrative of this essay.[5]

The widespread use of iron farming tools also makes evident that these diverse agriculturalists lived alongside a widely scattered group of artisans, sometimes existing side-by-side, or sometimes operating at great distances from each other. Most often they lived in different clans or ethnic groupings in different clusters of villages. In the midst of this

---

3   Rodney, *A History of the Upper Guinea Coast, 1545 to 1800*, 27 and 29.
4   Rodney, *A History of the Upper Guinea Coast, 1545 to 1800*, 27.
5   Rodney, *A History of the Upper Guinea Coast, 1545 to 1800*, 24–25. According to Rodney, the Djolas were the most effective producers of rice, the Balantas specialized in the farming of yams, the Banhuns produce millet, all of the afore mentioned ethnic groups also were effective producers of cows and goats in significant numbers. Other coastal distinctive communities had limited mixed horticultural success and had very few cows and goats if at all.

dynamic production of diverse products for immediate use and the development of a complex system of exchange for wider distribution, there also emerged a clan of artisan boat builders. These were the Mandinka (also called Mandingo), who eventually developed into a clan of itinerate traders. Originating within Mali, the Mandinka were able to maintain some of their institutional organization from the previous period.[6] They settled along the banks of the large rivers, where a natural profusion of huge trees provided them with the materials they used to refine their boat-building skills. By acquiring control over the mining and sale of salt (and to a lesser extent, gold) over time, they stimulated trade in agricultural and other commodities, which they transported via the network of rivers using their well-built and large canoes. These markets had their medium of exchange in precise, discreet denominations of salt and in gold. It was through the agency of the Mandinka, along with other ethnic groups gradually becoming involved in this multilevel and multi-dimensional production and trade, that these regional markets were integrated into the complex system of exchange that the Portuguese found operating along the coast. Doubtless, the Portuguese were unaware of the breadth of this trade, which extended deep into the interior.

From tightly knitted kinship-based clans to small diverse villages and larger hierarchical societies, there existed a complex mixture of social formations scattered throughout Africa's western coastal region. Contained within this evolving configuration was a multilayered and interconnected series of intimate and directly democratic political institutions, which took the form of self-organized decision-making councils that could be found in communities across the length and breadth of the region and served as the political compliment to this system of production and trade. There were village "chiefs" that made decisions in consultation with a council of elders. Depending on the local and regional circumstance, the council would directly govern or serve in an advisory role. It was as though the smaller size of the villages that were created during this period was driven by conscious human choice. The size and scale of the average village provided for the kind of intimate social contact that allowed for face-to-face decision making by people in the community, which in turn led to greater community self-management.

---

6   Rodney, *A History of the Upper Guinea Coast, 1545 to 1800*, 35.

Make no mistake, these large numbers of diverse villages and towns also provided a greater opportunity for the development of more rigidly organized hierarchies, revealing themselves in clans with hereditary lineages and outsized influence across the larger federation. Often, Eurocentric and elitist Afrocentric writers mistakenly describe some of the social formations of this region as being ruled by a "nobility." Sometimes these writers describe influential members of the community as "kings" with complete autocratic power. This is a common mistake given the historic involvement of these communities with the larger states of the Western Sudan and the legacy that lingered within these social formations as communities migrated toward the coast during the decline of those states.

There were certainly some villages that were organized in an autocratic fashion, but prior to European contact the vast majority of people that inhabited the western coastal region lived in what could accurately be defined as stateless societies.[7] As the caustic and disorienting effects of the slave trade deepened, a layer of what might be called "nobility" did appear. They were the Indigenous "royalty" attached to the European merchants of the coast, and of course, they did not sell themselves into slavery. Consequently, the often-told story of enslaved African people in the Americas being the descendants of the great "kings and queens" of Africa is, by most research-based accounts, a myth.

The concept of an overarching aristocracy or a landed gentry with a monopoly ownership of the land and direct control of the agricultural production did not, for the most part, exist within the Guinea Coast region prior to the Trans-Atlantic Slave Trade. There were, however, traditional kinship-based societies with their own hierarchies, which could be said to have been crystalizing into classes—a process that was accelerated by the slave trade itself. These clans, classes, and stratum created a toxic mixture alongside the slave-trading middle merchants, turning the African continent inside out. But, again, the layers and classes that benefited from this human trafficking did not usually sell themselves or other members of their class or stratum into slavery.

---

7   Sam Mbah, *African Anarchism: The History of a Movement* (Tuscon: See Sharp Press, 1997), 27–38.

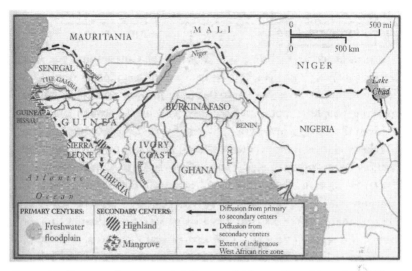

Figure 10. Centers of origin and diffusion of African Rice. Note that diffusion of rice cultivation roughly followed the diffusion of Mande-speaking peoples toward the coast, as seen in Figure 9. Source: Jane Landers, *Black Rice*, Figure 2.1.

ECOLOGICAL IMPLICATIONS OF RICE PRODUCTION ON THE GUINEA COAST

Western Africa's wide-ranging and dynamic network of social institutions was largely entangled with the production and distribution of food. Rice, yams, and millet were the primary food staples. Of these, rice proved to be the most significant and its widespread cultivation among western African villages was of crucial historical importance. The sale of limited rice surpluses by local villages to itinerate "merchants" and its consumption played a unifying economic and cultural role. Importantly, this crop was *not* produced by a few wealthy farmers as a cash crop for a large market. It was produced by a multitude of small farmers for mostly local trade and consumption. Only a small amount of rice production was intended for wider trade and the scale of production, trade, and consumption of rice was limited enough to allow a certain degree of self-management in this collective enterprise.

As the cultivation of rice developed over time, ecological and agricultural knowledge became more generalized and specific cultivation methods evolved to cope with certain challenges. For instance, in the case of coastal "swamp rice"—which became the region's predominant variety of rice because of its greater yield and its easier integration into coastal ecosystems—desalination and drainage control were the most obvious and immediate problems to be solved. Meeting these challenges required a precise timing of crop cycles to coincide with the tides, as well as the preservation of the coastal landscape for the continued sustainability of crops into the future. Seasonal flooding and heavy rainfall during certain months also had to be considered.[8] As a result of the enormous knowledge gained through the practical experience in the long-term production of rice and other crops, a profound understanding of local and regional ecologies grew by leaps and bounds.

Although some communities became more proficient at growing rice, this knowledge was never monopolized by any one clan, class, or ethnic group. This was communal knowledge that emerged horizontally through cooperation and was shared among the people in quite the same way. It is also important to remember that rice was never a European crop in any sense. It was, in every sense, an African agricultural staple and food crop that emerged from the brilliant creativity, ingenuity, and labor of ordinary people living in diverse African communities.

---

8   Walter Rodney, *A History of the Upper Guinea Coast, 1545 to 1800*, 20–21. For an in-depth study of the social-ecological development of rice cultivation, see also: Judith Carney, *Black Rice: The African Origins of Rice Cultivation in the Americas* (Cambridge: Harvard University Press, 2001).

CHAPTER 8.
THE IMPACT OF COLONIAL RICE PRODUCTION

The coastal lowcountry of what is now South Carolina and Georgia is and was remarkably similar to the Guinea Coast of Africa. In terms of climate and ecology, these two coasts were almost mirror images of each other. Both possessed an abundance of tidal-influenced rivers and creeks. In both regions there exists a critical supply of freshwater from a predictable upcountry seasonal rainfall upon a relatively flat and wide coastal plain with lowland swamps. This was the type of landscape on which African farmers had cultivated rice for generations.

In the Americas, kidnapped, trafficked, and enslaved African laborers were violently forced to produce the very same crop on a much larger and ever-growing scale. Therein lay the critical distinction. In Africa the crop was relied upon as food for those who produced it, as well as for distribution and consumption within essentially limited local markets. Hence, the scale of its production, in that context, did not devastate the ecological landscape to the degree that it would in the Carolinas. In addition, the form, rapidity, and general direction of the knowledge associated with its cultivation was contained within a manageable scale. This was not to be in South Carolina.

By the late seventeenth century, knowledge of rice production had been transferred from Africa to the Carolinas. By the 1690s, rice was being exported as a cash crop and shortly thereafter, in the 1720s, it had become the largest commodity produced for international sale from the

Carolina colony.[1] The region's growing demand for rice and its highly technical cultivation laid the developmental basis for a complex society that relied entirely upon enslaved labor. In 1703 the enslaved African population of the South Carolina colony was approximately three thousand. By 1720 it grew to twelve thousand. By 1739 it had ballooned to twenty-nine thousand, greatly outnumbering the European population of the colony.[2] A large portion of this laboring population was conscripted into rice cultivation. In fact, Africans were selected for enslavement from regions in Africa known for their knowledge and skill in the production of rice and related agricultural products.[3]

Rice produced in the Carolinas, and later in Georgia, required intense and concentrated labor, imprisoned within an enormous enslaved-labor farm system that was constantly increasing in size, scope, and number. This system, which was created to produce a for-profit cash crop on an ever-growing commercial and international scale, was inherently unstable and ecologically unsustainable. This dehumanized labor, organized and enforced by the weight of shackles and the ever-present sting of the lash, was resisted in every way possible—and impossible—by its human victims.

The enslaved-labor farms (often called "plantations") on the rice coasts of South Carolina and Georgia were merely one example of the widespread use of enslaved labor in pre-industrial North American capitalism, but they are of great importance to our study of Fort Mose because the early inhabitants of Mose represented a particular moment in the generalized resistance to this oppression. They came to Spanish Florida directly from the rice-growing region of South Carolina.

It must be emphasized again and again, that this enslaved labor, accumulated as living capital, allowed for the creation of surpluses that formed the basis for the Industrial Revolution in Western Europe and the northeastern United States. Put more directly, it was the protracted exploitation of enslaved Africans that allowed for the emergence of the modern world that we know today. The accumulation of these huge material surpluses

---

1   Judith Carney, *Black Rice: The African Origin of Rice Cultivation in the Americas*, (Cambridge: Harvard University Press, 2001), 84–85.
2   Carney, *Black Rice*, 87–89.
3   Carney, *Black Rice*, 4.

came directly from the large-scale enslavement of captive human beings from the societies of western and central Africa, who were themselves following their own unique developmental trajectories prior to the disruptive effects of their catastrophic enslavement. It was they who were the most indispensable part of these emerging colonial empires centered in western Europe and later in New England. Huge amounts of this conscripted labor were converted quite literally into a large proportion of pre-industrial capital.[4] Not only were these persons physically dehumanized and transformed into capital themselves, but their scientific, technical, and ecological knowledge was also appropriated in a violent and coercive social exchange that was unequal, oppressive, and exploitative in every way. This labor, along with stolen Indigenous land—usually granted to settlers by some European state official—was used for the production of cash crops and mining operations in the colonial period, suppling an ever-expanding and differentiated world market.

In many instances, this official authority took the form of joint stock companies operating either independently or through the Crown of one of the European powers.[5] These primitive companies and emerging state formations represented the beginnings of what would become the monstrously large international corporations and hyper-militarized nation states that we know today. An unbridled search for profits and the European settlement that facilitated this exploitation became the most defining feature of the social, ecological, and geopolitical landscape of the Americas, most definitively in the southeastern region of North America, where enslaved-labor farms became the most viable and therefore the most prevalent context for the brutal exploitation of captive African laborers.

As the thirst for new land and more profits fueled the expansion of this system, so continued the protracted genocidal war against Indigenous peoples and the widespread destruction of the region's natural ecology. So too did the human resistance to this immoral rampage persist. It was

---

4 Modibo M. Kadalie, *The Independent African American Labor Movement in the Formation of the American State and the Consolidation of American Capitalist Class Power,* Ph.D. Dissertation, (Atlanta: Atlanta University, 1989).

5 These joint stock companies went by such names as The Virginia Company of London (1606–1624) and the Royal African Company (1672–1752), among others.

resisted from within by enslaved Africans, and it was resisted from the outside by Indigenous peoples. This resistance took many forms and revealed itself with deadly intensity from generation to generation as it persisted throughout the centuries. Fort Mose was the manifestation of this resistance that emerged in a very small, yet very significant place for one moment in history.

THE EMERGENCE OF MAROON COMMUNITIES

Fort Mose was an autonomous maroon community among a profusion of maroon communities scattered throughout the regions of the new world, especially in areas where for-profit monocrop agriculture predominated. Autonomous maroon communities emerged to challenge the oppressive enslaved-labor farming system wherever the conditions of captive labor existed in the Americas. Some of these communities have been documented; others have been lost to history. These previously enslaved fugitives, driven by their own freedom-seeking impulse, created communities of resistors and became the most viable form of collective and sustained institutional rebellion against rapidly spreading colonial settler-states and commercial capitalism in its infancy. The establishment and the existence of these distinctive communities demonstrated that the Trans-Atlantic trade in enslaved people was more than a relocation of a highly skilled laboring population; it was also the forced transfer of diverse peoples who held an extensive living social memory.

Major long-term maroon communities sprang up in regions of the South American mainland that we now call Brazil, Colombia, Ecuador, Guyana, and Suriname. Other such communities emerged on the larger islands of the Caribbean that we now call Hispaniola, Cuba, Jamaica, Puerto Rico as well as some of the smaller islands.[6] There were also large and influential maroon communities on the North American mainland, principally in southeastern Mexico in what is now the State of Vera Cruz, and within the southeastern region of the United States, in areas we now call Florida, Georgia, South Carolina, North Carolina, and coastal

---

6 For perhaps the most well documented of these protracted movements of resistance is chronicled in C.L.R. James, *The Black Jacobins: Toussaint L'Ouverture and the San Domingo Revolution* (New York: Random House, 1963).

Virginia. These communities of freedom seekers sprang up within the mountainous interiors of large Caribbean islands, in frontier areas far from the coast, deep within swamps or in places where European colonial power was contested, weak, or did not yet reach at all. Depending on the specific politics and conditions of any particular colonial oppressor at any given period in time, these communities were sometimes vastly different from one another, tending to vary in form, location, duration, size, complexity, and degree of independence.

At first, early populations of self-emancipated Africans were simply absorbed into existing Indigenous communities after they escaped slavery. Most of these communities were brutally repressed, decimated by colonial militias, with many of their inhabitants murdered in much the same manner as other Indigenous communities, but this was not always the case. Some of the larger, more remote and inaccessible maroon societies even signed written treaties or reached agreements that allowed them to co-exist alongside European settlements and enslaved-labor farms.[7]

An understated but common attribute that many of these communities had with each other was that they demonstrated a dynamic interconnectivity with their immediate natural surroundings. This was more apparent in maroon communities, who lived with a greater degree of autonomy from the enslaved-labor farm system, from which they had escaped. In many ways, the maroons were consciously fashioning an alternative, more ecological, and more communalistic social life.

There are many recorded instances of failed attempts at European settlement because of colonialists' inability to cope with local ecologies. Where successful European settlement did eventually occur, it was often with the benevolent assistance of local Native peoples. Seldom did maroon communities fail because of their inability to successfully interact with their natural environment. In fact, they often chose out of necessity to settle in regions that were hostile to the encroachment of Europeans.

Even though maroon communities were under a constant state of siege from European colonial powers, they nevertheless managed to

---

7 The most well-known examples are the Jamaican maroon treaties of 1739 and 1740. For a closer study of these treaties see Mavis C. Campbell, *The Maroons of Jamaica, 1655–1796* (Trenton: Africa World Press, 1990).

organize themselves in a manner that allowed individuals to collectively influence the important decisions of their society. These societies, large and small, were made up primarily of West Africans and were culturally West African (as much as the immediate ecological context would allow).

It is important to recall that African societies from the Guinea Coast—from where so many of these maroons had been forcibly displaced—were generally less rigid, less hierarchical, more ecological, and more egalitarian than the societies of their European oppressors. In a very real sense, their social and ecological worldview was more akin to that of North America's Indigenous communities than it was to that of their European captors, who came from developing nation-states marked by rigidity, unequal social classes, and fixed roles based upon race, gender, and all manner of complex social and institutionalized relations of dominance and hierarchy. In such circumstances, simple human truths suffer. These types of social formations were hostile to ecology and European rulers generally saw themselves as ruling above nature.[8] Mastery or domination over nature was how human social development was measured by elites from those European societies where private property had emerged, and where the rabid scramble for wealth that defines the headlong ecological destruction that we know today as consumer capitalism finds its intractable origins.

RACIST LOGIC OF THE ENSLAVEMENT SYSTEM

As this clash of conflicting social systems continued to unfold, its deadly and destructive consequences began to exact a lasting effect within the Americas and Europe. A dominant narrative also emerged to justify the protracted carnage that continues to this day. Although African labor was never really stable within the enslaved-labor farming system (since it was constantly punctuated by rebellion after rebellion), it was, however, productive through the direct application of great coercive brutality. This system was just stable enough to yield huge profits from the sale of slave-produced commodities—derived from the ownership and control of enslaved Africans themselves as private property—on ever-expanding world markets.

---

8   Carolyn Merchant, *The Death of Nature: Women, Ecology, and the Scientific Revolution* (New York: HarperCollins, 1989), 127–140.

The basic logic that emerged to justify this long-term exploitation was as follows: Africans are not humans. They are property. They are not worthy of any kind of respect that might be afforded to the lowliest of Europeans. As property, they are incapable of reasoning and are therefore soulless beings. As such they are devils by nature. This classically racist conceptualization became imbedded within the popular culture of the times. In fact, we still confront it in the twenty-first century. Indigenous peoples were likewise considered to be primitive animals that resemble human beings but were incapable of understanding the concept of private property, which European colonizers considered to be a fundamental aspect of "civilization." They too were animalistic beings, soulless creatures, and devils. Indigenous peoples were also considered to be in the way of an expanding civilization and thus needed to be exterminated. These were the gross assumptions that underpinned the white supremacy of the times, perpetuated by an emergent racist narrative that was gradually being written into history.

There was, nevertheless, some debate within the narrow constraints of Christian ethics. Within this very limiting context, one question being debated was: are Natives and enslaved Africans so inhuman to the extent that they could not be saved by Christian baptism and Christian education? Some Europeans argued that since these people of color were inhuman, they simply had no soul to be saved. Their inhumanity and inherent evil were beyond the reach of Christian salvation. Other Europeans were of the belief that some Africans and Indigenous people could be saved by baptism and stern Christian indoctrination. There were many and various shades and derivations of responses to this basic question, all occurring within the constraints of the prevailing racist assumptions of the times, and recorded in the official policies, legal frameworks, and documents of the British, French, Spanish, and to a much lesser extent, the Portuguese and Dutch imperial governments. It goes without saying, that the implementation of *any* imperialist state policies reinforced the male chauvinist, elitist, and racist assumptions of the time, thereby cementing into being a most intractably violent and dangerous dogma which seemed to be preordained and unalterably obvious to all who believed it.

This ideological conceptualization persists through the primary source documents used uncritically by most historians to develop their inaccurate descriptions of the period.[9] The widespread and deepening assumption of this racist narrative also fundamentally took for granted that the Americas were "virgin" lands, scarcely inhabited by uncivilized—sometimes noble, sometimes ignoble—savages and Africa was a "dark continent" inhabited by a large number of lesser human animals (or devils) who were incapable of being civilized. Therefore, it was the alleged responsibility of the white race to use these people for "God's" purpose. Of course, God, understood by settlers as a kind of supernatural and universal European landlord, ordained the white race to steal and profit from the lands of Indigenous peoples and the skilled labor of enslaved Africans. This was accepted as "common sense" among all layers of European colonial society at the time and was the context for the emergence of white chauvinism. As a matter of fact, the idea of the existence of "white people," collectively considered across classes, was the exception to the rule prior to this time.

It is perhaps not surprising then, that while historians have long acknowledged the existence of maroon communities throughout the Americas since the time of European colonization, there has been no real systematic study of their internal self-governing dynamics. The chapters that follow attempt to contribute some small effort toward the study of how these autonomous communities organized themselves and collectively sustained their societies, and the creative manner in which they interacted with each other and with the rest of nature during the period under consideration.

---

9   Records of the Catholic Church, as well as other church records, were also relied upon. It goes without saying that the racial, class, and ethnic assumptions and assertions of these sources must be considered in our evaluation of their reliability; and it is obvious that the general hierarchical, class specific, white supremacist, and misogynist structures of these institutions makes their record keeping suspect in every significant way.

CHAPTER 9.
A PLACE TO BE WHO WE ARE

Fort Mose was created organically from a conscious community of self-emancipated Africans who came to St. Augustine as the result of their long trek to escape from bondage in the British settler colony of Carolina. In the collective act of leaving Carolina, they were asserting their humanity and their freedom. The journey itself was an intensive search for a place where their freedom and self-emancipation could be achieved by finding a location where they could exercise their collective authority on their own terms. By leaving the hellish places of their bondage, they were literally saving their own lives and bequeathing unto their children the possibility of a fully realized humanity in all of its implied dimensions.

They brought with them their collective consciousness, derived from their lived personal and collective experiences and histories prior to being captured from their native land and forced, against their will, onto slave ships and carried across an ocean to a strange place and sold into a dehumanizing enslavement. Much of their humanity was forcibly taken from them when they became the property of others. So, in a most fundamental sense, escaping the Carolina colonies was necessary in order to reassert their humanity and their ownership of themselves.

This conscious act of resistance was not, at first, informed by knowledge that Spanish-held territories to the south would allow them to reestablish their lives as human beings. It merely allowed for the possibility. It was only later that the Spanish, acting under pressure from the many African refugees arriving from the British colonies, actually developed a policy of active manumission.

Africans' dynamically expanding and collectively conscious social movement was expressed in ever increasing numbers of fugitives throughout the region and the emergence of ever more complex and varied maroon communities. As this historical period unfolded over time, networks of enslaved and free African people acquired and communicated new knowledge that Spanish colonial policy allowed for their potential emancipation by a professed public acceptance of the Catholic faith. Implicit within this Spanish policy was an official acknowledgement of African people's souls. This was an institutional acknowledgement of African humanity to the world, affirmed by the religious practice of baptism, demonstrating that some degree of human social equality for Africans was now generally recognized within the limited boundaries of Spanish Florida. As early as 1555 in Cuba, 1557 in Puerto Rico, and in 1560 and 1572 in Cartagena, as well as in 1583 in Santo Domingo; the Spanish used free and enslaved Africans and Mulattoes in their organized militias in defense of their Caribbean possessions.[1] In fact, it was generally known that militiamen, soldiers, and sailors of African descent and mixed race "mulattoes" were well represented in all branches of the Spanish military throughout the Caribbean and the rest of the Spanish empire in the "new world." Even raiding privateers in the service of both the British and Spanish relied upon sailors and soldiers of African descent to man their ships as they plundered one another for gold, silver, and slaves, on the open seas. We might recall the English pirate, Sir Frances Drake, who relied upon a crew made up of a large number of Africans to prey upon Spanish fleets and inland shipments of gold and silver from Peru through Panama.[2]

DISTINCTIONS BETWEEN BRITISH AND SPANISH ENSLAVEMENT POLICY

While slavery existed in all of its brutality within Spanish colonial territories, there were some variations. Spanish colonial policy differed

---

1   Jane Landers, *Black Society in Spanish Florida*, (Urbana: University of Illinois Press: 1999), 22–23.
2   Miranda Kaufmann, "The Untold Story of How an Escaped Slave Helped Sir Francis Drake Circumnavigate the Globe" *History*. 12 January 2021. https://www.history.com/news/the-untold-story-of-how-an-escaped-slave-helped-sir-francis-drake-circumnavigate-the-globe.

from that of the English in particular regions where there was direct conflict with them or other empires. For the sake of a regional advantage during this period, the Spanish were willing to recognize the souls of Africans while the British were not. That is one reason why Fort Mose was a crucially significant place for Africans seeking freedom. They were actively pursuing their own humanity and, quite literally, searching for a place to reestablish their self-ownership after having been objectified as the private property of others. For one brief shining moment in time, Fort Mose became that place for these African freedom seekers. And because the Catholic church kept relatively meticulous records, many historians have asserted that Fort Mose was the "first" self-governing town of freed Africans in North America.

Important though it was, we must be careful about such assertions. It is perhaps more accurate to call Fort Mose the first *documented* self-governing town of self-emancipated Africans in the land that eventually (and regrettably) became known as the United States. Nevertheless, since we know that enslaved Africans have been leaving the places of their enslavement from their earliest arrivals at European settlements, there is no reason to exclude the probability of other earlier self-governing African communes in North America. Such settlements are, after all, well known in the histories of Mexico, of central and South America, and of the Caribbean archipelago.

Contrary to the dominant and bogus narrative that Fort Mose was built by the Spanish colonial government "for" African refugees from the English colonies, we must affirm that these freedom-seeking people created this sacred fortified place on their own authority. It was built by those who lived there, not by some policy initiative of the appointed Spanish Governor Manuel de Montiano. African people had come to St. Augustine, and the government needed to respond. Government policy does not create social movement; it is a response to it. So it was in the case of Fort Mose.

THE CAROLINA SETTLER COLONY

In 1670 when Charles Town was firmly established as a British colony with the arrival of the British planters from Barbados, the Carolinians began to contest Spanish rule of the coastal region north of the fledgling colony of Eastern Florida. Even though the town of St. Augustine was about three hundred miles down the coast (by land or sea) the Spanish Crown claimed the coast as far north as what is now Port Royal, South Carolina and just beyond.

These British Planters from Barbados had a vision of the Southeastern coast as a British-controlled, slave-owning, monocrop agricultural colony, but rice production had not yet become the dominant commodity. Even before the introduction of the large-scale rice cultivation, however, enslaved-labor farms were beginning to appear in the region, relying on the forced labor of imported Africans as well as that of Indigenous peoples. These plantations produced several other crops—indigo, sugar, some strains of cotton, and even some rice—but the Carolina colony was, at first, mostly engaged in the trade of animal furs and other commodities that were traded by Indigenous people for trans-shipment to Europe. These types of commercial activities yielded some surpluses, but the profit margins needed to maintain the level of investment from Europe to sustain the colony could not be achieved in this manner, and the Carolina settler colony floundered in its early years.

"Plantations" that relied upon enslaved African labor were nevertheless a fact of life from almost the very beginning of the English presence in the Carolinas. And the freedom-seeking response to this oppression was, therefore, also a part of this very early social history. In fact, the very first recorded wave of African freedom seekers coming to St. Augustine from the Carolina colony took place from 1688 to 1690, only eighteen years after the Charles Town colony was founded.

This early movement, followed by successive waves of self-emancipated people arriving from South Carolina undoubtedly made an impact on Spanish policies that governed the way in which freedom seekers from the north were to be handled. The dogged determination of the refugees from Carolina directly resulted in a policy shift in November 1693 that would affect the Spanish Caribbean for years to come. It is important to keep in mind, however, that the refugees were not so much coming to Spanish Florida as they were fleeing their bondage in South Carolina. That is an important distinction. The conscious exodus of African people pushed the Spanish authorities into a supportive position in which they eventually endorsed the subversive efforts of those Africans who had been enslaved in the rival British territories. The Spanish needed help to secure the Florida colony from British incursion. They had no choice but to allow African settlement. This theme continuously played out on the edges of contested European colonial borders throughout the so-called "new world."

Increased profitability of rice production quickly led to a dramatic expansion of the enslaved-labor farming system in the Carolinas, and later in Georgia, in order to accommodate emerging markets in Europe and elsewhere. Soon, the trade of Indigenous goods that possessed local-use value within and between Indigenous communities almost completely collapsed. And simultaneously, the fur trade between Native people from the interior and European settlements began to become less important in the commercial development of the region. With the advent of large-scale production of rice and the proliferation of private ownership of property, the pre-colonial trading patterns of Indigenous populations became subordinated to capitalist trade, under the control of European merchants in Charles Town. As a result, more violent clashes of settler militias with Native peoples—and of Native peoples with each other (allied or in opposition with various capitalist interests)—became part of an avaricious interior expansion of European settlement and the devastation of the social ecology of the region.[3]

In the northern coastal zone of the Carolina colony, which is today the border region of North Carolina and southeastern Virginia, there was a bitter conflict. From 1711 until 1715, well-armed militias from the English colonies and their Native allies fought against an Indigenous alliance coordinated largely by the Tuscaroran people in their own homeland. This is recorded in history as the "Tuscarora War," which, as we discussed in Part One, was a militant struggle against the alienation of Native lands and the capture and sale of Native women and children into slavery.[4] It

---

3   Cormac O'Brien, *The Forgotten History of America: Little-Known Conflicts of Lasting Importance from the Earliest Colonists to the Eve of the Revolution* (New York: Crestline, 2008) 197–200.

4   This war was fought in Eastern North Carolina from 22 September 1711 to 11 February 1715. The belligerents on one side were: the colonial militias of Carolina and Virginia; the Yamasee; the Apalachee; the Catawbas; the Cherokees; and the Northern Tuscarora. On the other side were the Southern

also was well known that the Tuscarora harbored African fugitives from slavery and included entire maroon communities among their ranks. The settlers wanted these lands to accommodate their expanding tobacco production and other lesser cash crops, all of which were produced using enslaved African labor. Conflicts like this one followed a pattern marked by shifting alliances and increased in frequency as time passed and the conflicts intensified.

An important and often overlooked consequence of the increased production of rice in South Carolina and tobacco in Virginia, as well as other supportive commodities and services this period of intensified colonial expansion, was the increased need for labor. African people with knowledge about any aspect of rice agriculture were especially sought after and targeted for enslavement during this period.

Between 1702 and 1704, the South Carolina settlers under the leadership of the slave-merchant Governor James Moore, conducted a vicious campaign to accomplish two objectives: 1) increase the profitability of the colony by augmenting the enslaved population; and 2) expand and consolidate English settlement via the enslaved-labor farming system in order to reduce the threat from the Spanish colony at St. Augustine, which by that time was following an open policy of granting freedom to enslaved persons who took refuge in the Florida territory.

During the next few years, the numbers of enslaved African laborers dramatically increased and, by 1708, they outnumbered the white population. As a result, the Carolina colony was rocked by slave revolts in 1711 and again in 1714. Many African fugitives left these enslaved-labor farms in 1715 and joined the indigenous Yamasee community in their war against the British colony. Prior to this time, the Yamasee maintained a tentative alliance with the British colonialists. They participated in slave trade and the fur trade. After repeated betrayals by the settlers, however, the Yamasee and their allies changed their position on slavery and aligned themselves with African fugitives fleeing oppression. This was a dramatic shift. During the recently-concluded Tuscarora War, they had been aligned with the English settlers against a Native population who were

---

Tuscarora, the Pamlico, the Cothechney, the Coree, the Neusiok, the Mattamuskeet and the Matchepungo.

seeking to maintain the integrity of their society in the face of destructive slavery and violent alienation from their lands. Now, the Yamasee found themselves in open conflict with their former allies, who were now seeking to expand their presence in the upcountry region of South Carolina.[5]

Conceptually, it is important to view the Tuscarora War and the Yamasee War as different phases of the same regional conflict. It really was the same war: a generalized war of Indigenous resistance. Although this uprising was defeated, it represents a successful coalition of African fugitives with an Indigenous resistance force, fighting a common struggle against enslavement itself and the ongoing war of Native genocide. Had these defensive wars of Native resistance been successful, they may have altered the course of history in the southeastern region for years to come.

THE ESTABLISHMENT OF FORT MOSE

After the Yamasee War, the Yamasee and the Africans moved south into a contested zone to which the Spanish were making a claim, just north of their colonial administrative center of St. Augustine. By 1728 a Black militia was organized at St. Augustine by formerly enslaved Africans who had fought in the Yamasee War. The militia helped to defend St. Augustine against a British invasion led by Colonel John Palmer in 1728. The Africans were reportedly led by a man who self-identified as an ethnic Mandingo. He eventually became known as Francisco Menendez and is credited for having led an Afro-Indigenous militia on raids against British-held territory claimed by Spain, acquiring white scalps and rescuing enslaved Africans. Most of these raids and small-scale military engagements—which were themselves a continuation of the generalized war of anti-colonial resistance—took place in the region between the Carolina colony and Spanish-held eastern Florida. The region eventually became the buffer colony of Georgia. During these raids, Menendez officially remained an enslaved person, but he continuously petitioned for

---

5   This war was fought primarily in the South Carolina upcountry from 14 April 1715 until the summer of 1717. The belligerents on one side were: the colonial militias of South and North Carolina, and Virginia, The Catawba joined in 1715, the Cherokee joined in 1716. On the other side the Yamasee, the African enslaved maroons, the Ochese Creeks, the Waxhaw, and the Santee. The Catawba left the coalition in 1715, and the Cherokee left the coalition in 1716.

Figure 11. An artists' reconstruction of Fort Mose featured on a historical marker at the Fort Mose Historic State Park.

his freedom and that of his men. It was not until 15 March 1738 that the petitioners were granted their official emancipation by the pragmatic colonial Governor Manuel de Montiano, who was faced with a continuing influx of African fugitives arriving from the north.

The African community to which Menendez belonged established themselves in a town called Mose, two miles north of St. Augustine. In a letter to the Spanish king, Governor Montiano renamed the town Gracia Real de Santa Teresa de Mose, crediting the crown with its establishment and adorning it with the name of Spain's patron saint, Teresa of Ávila. Mose itself, however, had already been established before its official Spanish naming. In fact, the name "Mose" is derived from "Musa," the Arabic name for Moses, indicating that this self-organized African maroon community was both established and named by its African residents themselves and that this name was reflected in the record of Spanish authorities, even if it was mispronounced.[6]

The town was fortified and served as a defensive outpost for nearby St. Augustine. Its walls were constructed of stone and earth. A shallow

6   Samory Rashid, *Black Muslims in the U.S.: History, Politics, and the Struggle of a Community,* (New York: Palgrave Macmillan, 2013) 48–49.

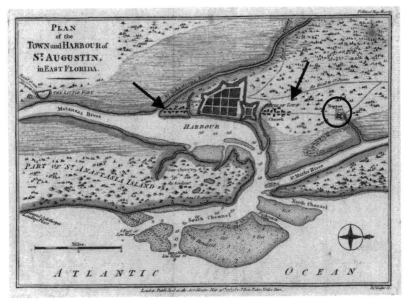

Figure 12. "Plan of the Town and Harbor of St. Augustin, in East Florida, 1783." Fort Mose (right), labeled as "Negroe Fort," is circled. Note also the two "Indian towns" (center and left) established outside of St. Augustine.

moat filled with cacti surrounded the fort on all sides. A church, a well, and several palm-thatched houses designed in a West African style were built inside of the walls. Outside more houses could be found, surrounded by fields of food crops.[7] Mose was a place of natural abundance, built on fertile soil near a saltwater river where residents could harvest fish and shellfish. The people of Mose traded and otherwise intermingled on a daily basis with the people of St. Augustine and nearby Indigenous communities, but at any given time about one hundred Africans lived at the fort.

Earlier, in 1703, Spanish efforts at the colonialization of western Florida had been almost defeated by a military incursion led by the former British governor and Carolina plantation owner, James Moore, but the Spanish were so far successful in asserting their presence in the region. In an attempt to block the Spaniards' westward push from the eastern

---

7   Landers, *Black Society in Spanish Florida*, 15.

coast of Florida, the British attempted to build a fort to the west, along the Apalachee River (near what is now Tallahassee), during the summer of 1739. They used enslaved African labor. In a previous military action in 1704, over a hundred Indigenous people local to the region were taken to Carolina and enslaved alongside an additional 1,300 captive Apalachee who were resettled in the Carolina upcountry in order to create a buffer of supportive Natives against the growing hostility of the Yamasee and other societies in the region. These acts of displacement and ethnic cleansing resulted in the depopulation of northeastern-central Florida and the opening up of the region for the establishment of British settler monocrop plantations. There were simply not enough Natives remaining to undertake the fort construction in 1739, even if they had been enslaved. The British effort proved to be a catastrophic failure. In August 1739 the entire English population was killed in a rebellion and over a hundred Africans escaped to the west, to the southeast, and to St. Augustine.[8]

The very next month, 9 September 1739, a revolt of enslaved Africans in Stono, South Carolina killed over twenty British Colonialists, sending shock waves through the territory. Many of the rebels were caught and executed, but many more went south, also traveling to St. Augustine.[9]

After establishing a settlement south of the Altamaha River delta at Fort Frederica—on the northwestern tip of what is now St. Simons Island—in an attempt to consolidate the new colony of Georgia along the Atlantic Coast, the British launched yet another attack on St. Augustine in May of 1740. The British forces, led by James Edward Oglethorpe, attacked from the north and were met with fierce resistance.

---

8   Landers, *Black Society in Spanish Florida*, 34.

9   While the insurrection of enslaved people in the Western Hemisphere was not a rare occurrence, there were some that were recorded and others that went unrecorded. The Stono Revolt was among those that were recorded. Further, at different periods of African enslavement, self-organized escape routes (or "underground railroads") extended in many different directions. During the period under our consideration, freedom seekers typically went south. During the pre-Civil War period, they typically went north. During the Reconstruction period, they went west; but always these routes traveled away from those areas where state power was most concentrated, and those areas that were most quickly becoming what we now know as the United States of America.

The people of the first Fort Mose settlement were evacuated south to St. Augustine's enormous walled fort, Castillo de San Marcos, in the face of the attack. A month-long siege of St. Augustine ensued. Two weeks into the siege, the British attempted to breach the walls with a focused and concentrated assault. This assault was repelled by a Spanish force led by Fort Mose's Black militia. Their resolve was undoubtedly fueled by the very real fear that, were they to fail, they would again be captured, sold, and re-enslaved in the English colonies. The British assault was beaten back and the fighting spirit of the Black militia was revealed for all to see. It was at this point that the legend of Francisco Menendez began to take shape.

By 17 May 1740 the Spanish forces were able to gather themselves within the city and mount a counter-attack, breaking the siege, and retaking an almost completely destroyed Fort Mose. This was a combined Spanish, African, and Indigenous force, in which Francisco Menendez's militia was the vanguard. The British lost approximately seventy-five soldiers and suffered a humiliating defeat. With the eventual arrival of reinforcements from Cuba and the fear of an approaching storm, a substantially weakened British force withdrew. This battle came to be known as "Bloody Mose."[10]

Emboldened by this success, Spanish military commanders in Cuba saw the possibility of taking the British settler town at Fort Frederica and reestablishing a Spanish presence in Georgia. They thought that a swift counter-attack against a weakened force might prove successful. The reinforcements that had arrived from Cuba, along with the destabilizing efforts of African freedmen fighting among the enslaved populations at the plantations in advance of the main military assault, were central to their calculations.[11] The plan relied upon the English-speaking Africans spreading the promise of freedom and land as they hoped to arm and recruit other enslaved people to join the Spanish forces in an insurrection against the British colony's slaveowners. On 7 July 1742 the Spanish

---

10   Landers, *Black Society in Spanish Florida*, 27.

11   According to Jane Landers (p. 38), the Spanish fighting force consisted of about one thousand regulars, both African and Mulatto; twenty-four African and Mulatto officers; 468 men from the Cuban militia, both African and Mulatto; and approximately one hundred Africans from St Augustine.

military engaged the British in what became known as "the Battle of Bloody Marsh" across the marshes of southeastern St. Simon Island, but suffered a defeat and quickly withdrew to St. Augustine. For the remainder of 1742 and 1743, the British continued to unsuccessfully attack St. Augustine. In the midst of what amounted to a protracted stalemate, enslaved Africans continued traveling to Florida in an ongoing migratory stream.

From the foregoing we can see that the decades between 1733 and 1763 were marked by a confluence of historical processes. The southern spread of British settler colonialism also marked the spread of rabid capitalism and ecological devastation, manifested in the form of coastal rice plantations. This spread resulted in increased pressure on the Spanish military, who were growing increasingly more reliant upon the Black militia in Florida, which offered the stiffest resistance to the British expansion southward.

Within this contested zone comprising coastal Georgia and northeastern Florida, the Spanish tactic of destabilizing the British colonial plantation system by encouraging enslaved Africans to flee south was a defining aspect of this dynamic historical period. These efforts at destabilization were accomplished primarily through the Black militia, which was comprised of guerilla fighters who could speak several African and Indigenous languages, as well as Spanish and English, and could help facilitate their escape to freedom.

On the other hand, the British sought to expand their enslaved-labor agriculture system by increasing their numbers of settlers through the use of land grants, and their Native allies by bolstering their military presence. This was the emerging and evolving face of European capitalist colonialism fighting back and forth in contestation within this geo-political region. These two colonizing empires were essentially locked in a stalemate for decades during the mid-eighteenth century. This was only one of the many flashpoints of the greater conflict between the British and the Spanish colonialists. At the same time, and within this same historical and political context, Indigenous peoples and self-emancipated Africans were creating and fashioning new and distinctive communities as they vigorously expressed their most advanced social selves.

CHAPTER 10.
THE ROLE OF FRANCISCO MENENDEZ

In the study of Fort Mose, no singular personality has become more significant to historians than that of Captain Francisco Menendez. While he is undoubtedly a figure of great importance, our present study seeks to avoid the veneration of any single individual within the context of unfolding historical events. History does not move at the whim of the individual, no matter how insightful, inspiring, or charismatic that person might be. Historically significant figures do, nevertheless, emerge from the evolving array of social institutions that exist in dynamic relations with one another at any given historical conjuncture. Their conscious living involvement with these institutions gives them their social significance, dynamism, and influence—some over a long period of time, others for a limited or singular moment.[1] In any event, it seems that Francisco Menendez remained significant to Fort Mose over a long period of time and within a number of successive historical contexts. This leads us to ask: Who was this African Mandingo with a Spanish name and title? How did he come to be known as "Captain Menendez?" How did his name become so prominently associated with Fort Mose?

At the risk of some repetition, let us review the context of his life and times. The first period of the existence of Fort Mose was brief, existing

---

1   Some historical figures, in fact, are very influential during one period in history and then totally irrelevant during the next. Ascendant rulers in one period, for example, often seek to elevate significant progressive figures from previous periods to positions of influence, even though their period of relevance has passed. This is typically done in order to legitimize the new hierarchy.

primarily as a military garrison from about 1738 to May of 1740, when it was evacuated as the siege of St. Augustine began. Even so, it was a community settled by freedom seeking people. It was physically constructed by them, and established and governed by them, at a location about two miles north of the Spanish colonial town of St. Augustine and nearby to several Indigenous towns with which it continued to be interrelated over time.

In 1740 the British, after having captured several small Spanish garrisons and missionary outposts along the St. John's River, turned a large assault force eastward toward St. Augustine. Fort Mose had already been destroyed and evacuated. The Black militia fought the attacking British forces alongside the rest of the people living within the town of St. Augustine. It was in this battle, which broke the British siege of St. Augustine, that the legend of Francisco Menendez was born.

Although the British attack was defeated for the time being, it was assumed that other attacks may be forthcoming. Fort Mose was too exposed and therefore vulnerable. Additionally, because of the fierce fighting prowess of the Black militia, St. Augustine could benefit from the additional protection that such a force offered. For the next twelve years, the Black militia of Fort Mose continued conducting their raids against British enslavement farms from their base in St. Augustine. Though not under the direct command of "Captain" Menendez, their efforts were partly inspired by his emerging legend.

Menendez was perhaps one of the most complex, enigmatic, and at the same time, significant historical figures of his time. Unfortunately, we have no record of his African name. We know that he was captured on the western coast of Africa at a young age. He derived his early socialization from the widespread trading community of the Mandingo people. Upon arrival in South Carolina in chains circa 1710, he was sold and most likely worked as an enslaved laborer on rice plantations for a brief but unspecified number of years. There were recorded revolts of enslaved people in the British Carolinas in 1711 and again in 1714, shortly after his arrival, and we have already discussed how the Carolina ecology and landscape was greatly similar to the physical environment of the Gambia River region of the upper Guinea Coast in Menendez's native Africa.[2] We can imagine

---

2   Landers, *Black Society in Spanish Florida*, 26.

that, as a young and brave Mandingo, he may have explored the ecological spaces that surrounded him. Of course, during this time, his name was not yet Menendez. That would come later.

After he escaped from the plantation, he went inland to fight with the Yamasee at about the same time that a significant number of Yamasee had abandoned their previous alliance with the British settlers and initiated an all-out war against them.[3] This intense conflict, known as the Yamasee War, lasted approximately two years (1715–1717) and pitted a regional alliance of Native towns and communities with the Yamasee at its core against the British colonial forces, their Indigenous allies, and even some enslaved people. During this time, the young Mandingo and other formerly enslaved Africans learned about the military tactics of the British as well as the communication skills necessary to facilitate the guerilla style military operations of the Yamasee and their allies against their common enemy. They also earned the respect of the Yamasee and the other Indigenous peoples involved in this conflict. After the British were successful in pitting these Indigenous communities against one another, causing Native alliances to weaken and fall apart, the Africans and the Yamasee withdrew to the south, across the Savannah River. They had become an integrated community and a unified fighting force that traveled together.

The popular narrative of these events describes a total defeat of the Yamasee and their African allies and their seeking the protection of the Spanish Crown in Eastern Florida. This, however, gives the Spanish too much credit. So too does the popular assumption that the Fort Mose militia was conscripted later, under Spanish authority. This fighting force, which historians have called the "Spanish Militia" or the "Black Militia" had already been formed long before 1727, when their initial contact with the Spanish occurred. It was an independent and unified armed force of Africans and Yamasee that conducted guerilla-style raids, freeing enslaved people from the plantations along the Edisto River and to the south as the Yamasee War came to an end.[4] There is an account of just such an independent military force made up of "ten Negroes and fourteen Indians

---

3   Landers, *Black Society in Spanish Florida*, 28.
4   Landers, *Black Society in Spanish Florida*, 27.

Commanded by those of their own Colour, without any Spaniards in company with them," attacking a Carolina ensalved-labor farm in 1727.[5]

It is not clear from our limited information, just exactly how these armed fighting forces organized themselves. We know that they were a small group, agile and effective—and they were not accompanied by any Spanish officers. This might imply a level of directly democratic consensus in their decision making and a leadership chosen by popular consensus. [6]Through their successful destabilizing of British settler plantations within the region, they were fighting in defense of their own self-emancipation. They were so effective that the one Spanish Governor of St. Augustine, Antonio de Benavides, began to pay them for their raids.[7]

By now it should be clear that the Spanish did not organize the Black militia, they merely affirmed its preexistence and recognized its strategic value and incorporated it in their own overall defensive scheme. Compared to the British, the Spanish were in a substantially weakened position and were barely holding onto their Florida colony. Owing to their urbanized pattern of settlement, they actually controlled very little of Florida outside of St. Augustine proper.

The British colonies were more self-sufficient and less dependent upon supplies from England whereas the Spanish settlers were almost completely dependent upon supplies from Spain and Cuba. The British were aggressively extending their for-profit monocrop plantation system to the west, north and to the south with a constant fresh supply of subsidized settlers, plantation owners, and enslaved laborers. Their basic

---

5   Quoted in Landers, *Black Society in Spanish Florida*, 27.

6   Historian Marcus Rediker has written about the similar effectiveness of directly democratic self-organization among Atlantic pirates who sailed during the period 1717–1726. These independent seafaring fighting forces made all of their decisions by consensus in a "common council" of the ship. Officers were elected and commanded only very limited authority. It is perhaps not surprising, then, that Francisco Menendez and other fighters from Fort Mose would later pursue work as pirates. See: Marcus Rediker, *Villains of All Nations: Atlantic Pirates in the Golden Age* (Boston: Beacon Press, 2004), 63–71. (A.Z.)

7   The Spanish Governor paid thirty pieces of eight for each English scalp and one hundred pieces of eight for each live negro that they were able to deliver. It is interesting that they offered no payment for African or Indigenous scalps.

pattern of settlement was more rural. This allowed them to spread their population over a larger area even though there were also supportive urban commercial centers that emerged within British colonies.[8] In this way, they were able to pursue a vigorous trade in mostly slave-produced commodities with England and the rest of Europe. The Spanish relied largely upon Catholic missions and Native conversions for their expansion and their colonial effort became gradually weaker as a result of their ineffective patterns of settlement. Spanish missions were engaged in essentially subsistence production with a small volume of trade outside of the mission with Indigenous communities or with Spain and Cuba, mediated through St. Augustine.

The Black militia offered Spain a significant and much-needed resistance to the rapid expansion of British plantation settlements moving southward toward Florida. The same fighters who had escaped enslaved labor on British plantations and had fought against the British alongside the Yamasee, were now once again fighting against the British on the side of the Spanish. In these efforts, they reveal themselves to have been consistent fighters against slavery, driven by an unwavering desire for freedom.

During the decade between 1728 and 1738, the Black militia from St. Augustine made their raids upon the British plantations along Florida's northern and western frontiers. Francisco Menendez was beginning to develop a reputation for his tactical planning, fighting capability, knowledge of the environment, and bravery in battle. Over time he earned the respect of his fellow soldiers and a popular mandate for leadership, rooted in their trust. At some point during this period, he was baptized into the Catholic Church at St. Augustine and began to be addressed by the title "Captain" Menendez. As African fugitives began to increase their numbers in St. Augustine, the governor simply sent them to Captain Menendez to see after them. Thus, Menendez remained on the cutting edge of this widespread social movement, which defined this period of history.

The establishment of Fort Mose in May of 1738 presented Manuel De Montiano, the new Governor of Florida, with an opportunity to free

---

8   Charles Town, of course, proved to be the greatest example of these centers of commerce within the southernmost colonial region.

the members of the Black Militia, expand it, and to legitimize Menendez as the principal patron within the Fort Mose community. This sanctioning gesture solved two problems for the governor: 1) it provided a simple way for the new arrivals from the north to become part of this growing Spanish frontier community; and 2) it allowed for a more robust defense of St. Augustine and its surrounding perimeter satellite settlements made up of diverse and relatively autonomous populations of Africans and Indigenous peoples. These self-sustaining communities (they were not dependent upon supplies from Cuba or Spain as was St. Augustine), which were by this time scattered throughout what is now northern and central Florida, were flashpoints for conflict with British colonialists as the dramatic increases of the fugitive slave populations in the area had become a threat to the expanding British system of enslaved-labor farming.

From the perspective of the self-emancipated Africans, with Menendez acting as their patron or spokesperson, the establishment of an independent self-organized community was simply the manifestation and continuation of their decades-long freedom struggle. The Africans of Fort Mose had various degrees of literacy, but Menendez's petitions for freedom and his ongoing correspondence with the Spanish authorities appear in the official record, and this has been cited as one reason why historians tend to describe him as if he were a chief or authoritarian leader.

In order to fully grasp the individual roles of Fort Mose's inhabitants (as well as the overall social position that the community as a whole) played during the time of its existence, we must consider the source of the records and the assumptions and motivations of those who undertake to write its history. While it is clear that the Spanish considered Menendez to be an authoritarian executive of his people, it is entirely unclear how much—if any—coercive power he actually wielded over the Fort Mose community. Indeed, there is no evidence whatsoever of any punishment or even any censorship—harsh or mild—taking place within the militia or within the civic life of Fort Mose during this first period (1738–1740).

It is therefore, inaccurate for historians to describe this community of freedom-seeking, self-emancipated fugitives, who had already escaped the bondage of slavery, as being ruled by this singular figure or any other. It is likewise inappropriate for historians to accept at face value Spanish authorities' twisted interpretations of diasporic African self-government in their midst. Menendez's legitimacy was not derived from any rigid structural hierarchy. In fact, given the historical context of converging directly democratic traditions that we have already outlined in this study, it is perhaps more accurate to say that Fort Mose was an autonomous community constructed by self-emancipated Africans as a manifestation of their collective labor and of their collective will, aspiring to a greater understanding of social freedom while navigating the political and geographic landscape of Spanish colonialism from the vantagepoint of their own peripheral frontier society.

Without any evidence that Menendez's civil influence was derived from coercive authority or externally applied commandism, we might say that his legitimacy in leadership emerged similarly to that of the Mico in the Muscogee communities that we discussed earlier, derived from a combination of distinguishing qualities that he possessed and from which the entire community could benefit. He was literate, as evidenced by the numerous petitions that he filed for himself and others, as well as the many letters that he wrote to Spanish officials that became part of the public record; he was respected in his military standing as the ranking officer of record in the militia; and he was known by his long-standing reputation for focused dedication, bravery, and experience.

Francisco Menendez was certainly an inspiring individual, but he was one among equals in a community full of inspiring individuals. His presence should not diminish our understanding of Fort Mose's intimate and directly democratic social character.

CHAPTER 11.
LIVING IN ST. AUGUSTINE, 1740-1752

After the destruction of the first Fort Mose by the British, the inhabitants of the community lived within the culturally diverse Spanish settler colony of St. Augustine proper, from 1740 until 1752, at which time the fort was reconstructed and continued to exist until its residences were finally evacuated to Havana as a result of a new treaty between England and Spain in 1763. Captain Francisco Menendez was absent from Spanish Florida for most of these twelve years. He and others from Fort Mose found employment as privateers, raiding British merchant vessels off the coasts of North America, South America, and the Caribbean. Doubtless Menendez saw himself as asserting his freedom and continuing the struggle against the British slave trade.[1] During this time, he was captured, imprisoned, beaten, and re-enslaved by the British. But through it all, exhibiting his uncanny will to survive and his creative perseverance—likely along with some trickery—he eventually managed to return to St. Augustine in 1759 after this trying and adventurous period of his life. After nineteen years away, he was once again among the ranking officers in residence at Fort

---

1   As noted earlier, the profession of pirating or privateering during this period was a remarkably democratic endeavor in which ship captains were elected and held very little authority. Nearly all decisions faced by pirate crews were decided by collective deliberation and consensus. This directly democratic model of self-organization would have been familiar to Menendez and others from Fort Mose. Indeed, many Africans from the region joined up with pirate vessels. See: Marcus Rediker, *Villains of All Nations*, 54, 60–82. (A.Z.)

Mose. Just four years later, Fort Mose and St. Augustine were evacuated and all of Spanish Florida was seeded to the British.[2]

During the twelve years between the first Fort Mose settlement and the second, St. Augustine underwent significant social changes. Newly self-emancipated Africans continued to arrive from the colonies of South Carolina and now Georgia in greater volume and with increasing frequency. The Catholic Church, for its part, began to exercise a much greater influence within the social lives of this larger African fugitive population. While showing significant African cultural and religious retentions on the one hand, the Africans of Fort Mose were becoming more Spanish—and therefore more Catholic—on the other. This created a certain amount of tension between long-term residents who were more thoroughly Catholic and those who were more recent arrivals.[3]

It is important to consider that for hundreds of years, direct Iberian (Spanish and Portuguese) contact with northern and western Africa had exerted a long-term influence upon the development of Spanish feudal society. This protracted social interaction includes the period of Moorish Islamic control of the peninsula. This complex history of non-European influence is reflected within the racial relations of the Spanish colonies and frontier settlements. It is for this reason that racial distinctions as a manifestation of social class were not as distinctive as compared to those that abided within British frontier settlements. Compared to British colonial society, the social relations of St. Augustine appear, in some ways, to be more relaxed. But make no mistake, there were definitive hierarchies of race, class, and gender; and slavery was an inseparable part of both Spanish and Portuguese societies and their colonial possessions.[4]

Again, it must be emphasized that dominant cultural structures, practices, and values were zealously maintained within this context by an authoritarian and externally appointed civil governor and an equally authoritarian clergy. The Church, through its various institutional structures and practices, defined and legitimized the terms of acceptable individual conduct and social relationships within the so-called "civilized," or

---

2   Landers, *Black Society in Spanish Florida*, 42–45.

3   Landers, *Black Society in Spanish Florida*, 45–60.

4   Larry Eugene Rivers, *Slavery in Florida: Territorial Days to Emancipation* (Tallahassee: University of Florida Press, 2008), 4–6.

European-dominated, community of St. Augustine. The people of Mose had to navigate these social norms and relationships. Not just through baptism, but also through marriage and god-parentage, an ever-increasing number of African fugitives from the English slave-holding colonies gained acceptance and were integrated into the St. Augustine community with the approval of Spanish colonial authority.

A further and much more profound distinction between British enslavement policy and that of the Spanish is relevant here. By recognizing the humanity of enslaved persons, that is, that the enslaved had souls that could be rescued from evil by baptism, certain other social practices logically followed. Upon baptism they could marry and christianize their offspring. Therefore, Black families, which often contained both enslaved and free members, became relatively more stable within Spanish Florida. Contrast this to British slavery, in which wives, husbands, and children were often forcibly separated from one another, never to see each other again. White slave masters even enslaved their own biological children. This was all tolerated even within the rigid religious codes and ethics of the various branches of the Protestant Church. These ideas and practices were driven by an extremely aggressive, violent, and labor-intensive form of agricultural commercialism.

In Spanish Florida, however, African and mixed-race families with stable extended family ties, often supported by the salaries of the militiamen as well as some very limited commercial enterprise, allowed the African fugitives to gain a degree of social acceptability. This acceptability gave those who possessed it certain privileges. They had greater access to property ownership and greater prestige, influence, and station in the hierarchies of local life.[5] Again, the scale of commercial intercourse was drastically limited, both within St. Augustine itself and within the regional network of indigenous and maroon communities that were thinly spread throughout Spanish Florida. The Catholic Church continued to exert a significant degree of influence over this and almost all other aspects of social life, to a greater or lesser extent, within the region.

Archeological evidence shows that the communities of Indigenous peoples and African freedom seekers in Spanish Florida were largely

---

5   Rivers, *Slavery in Florida*, 4–6.

reliant upon nature for their basic subsistence. They were autonomous and almost completely self-sufficient.[6] That is to say, these communities relied less upon outside trade and support. This same evidence, including faunal collections, demonstrates that the Native community of Novembre de Dios, a substantial village and mission near the northwestern wall of St. Augustine, relied upon almost identical resources as did the residents of St. Augustine and Fort Mose during the periods of its existence.[7] They all cooked and ate the same food. They used the same implements, farmed the same crops, and fished the same surrounding waters in much the same manner. They practiced, with some variation, the same or a similar religion and spoke a similar set of languages. In short, they were becoming more culturally integrated in spite of larger ethnic, racial, and class divisions. There was also no prohibition against interracial marriages or informal miscegenation.

As a result of this ongoing dynamic social process during the twelve years that the Fort Mose community resided within St. Augustine, the Africans were becoming an integral part of an emerging creole culture. This new and genuinely diverse culture was centered within the walls of St. Augustine but also encompassed an amalgamation of more than seven Native populations in two principal villages that were settled in the immediate area.[8] Although most of the original residents of Fort Mose lived within the city of St. Augustine during this time, they nevertheless formed stable and enduring relationships with their neighbors in nearby Indigenous villages.[9]

---

6   Landers, *Black Society in Spanish Florida*, 55.
7   For a comparative treatment of the diets of St. Augustine and its surrounding Indigenous and African communities, see Elizabeth J. Reitz and Stephen L. Cumbaa, "Diet and Foodways of Eighteenth-Century Spanish St. Augustine," in Kathleen A. Deagan ed., *Spanish St. Augustine: The Archeology of a Creole Community* (New York: Academic Press, 1983), 151–185.
8   Landers, *Black Society in Spanish Florida*, 53.
9   Jane Landers records the official Spanish names of the two largest villages as Nuestra Señora de la Leche and Nuestra Señora de Tholomato, however these are likely the names of Spanish Catholic missions operating within the towns themselves. A 1771 map records the names of at least six Indigenous towns in the area surrounding St. Augustine: Casapullas, Tolomato, Palica, Potolaca, Nombre de Dios, and Nombre de Dios Chiquito. Today, the site of

This process was taking place to a lesser extent throughout the more peripheral regions of Spanish Florida. A network of Catholic missions had been maintained by Indigenous labor in some of the more remote areas. They continued to send some of their agricultural surplus, in the form of tribute, to the colonial administration at St. Augustine. It could therefore be argued that St. Augustine was being supported to some extent by unequal trade from the outlying Native communities. Even supplies from Cuba and Spain were not sufficient enough to allow St. Augustine to operate, in any way at any time, as a self-sufficient colonial town.

---

the Indigenous town of Tolomato is memorialized by a historical marker on Cordova Street in St. Augustine, which describes an "Indian village served by Franciscan priests" and asserts that "The Tolomato Indians were Guale refugees fleeing attacks on their mission village in South Georgia." See: *Gracia Real de Santa Teresa de Mose: A Free Black Town in Spanish Colonial Florida* (St. Augustine: St. Augustine Historical Society, 1992), 24. See also: "Tolomato Indian Village," *Historical Marker Database*. https://www.hmdb. org/m.asp?m=47389. Accessed 1 January 2022; "Spanish map of the Saint Augustine area."1771. State Archives of Florida, *Florida Memory*. https://www. floridamemory.com/items/show/33665, Accessed 1 January 2022. (A.Z.)

CHAPTER 12.
THE SECOND FORT MOSE

In 1752 the St. Augustine colony was declining to the point of outright desperation. Spanish settlements to the northwest were coming under attack by more aggressive Indigenous forces as new alliances emerged and Native communities became more rapidly integrated with one another. The principal source of this new and different realignment of Native populations to the west and toward the interior of what is now the Florida panhandle and southwestern Georgia was the southward movement of the Oconee from areas we now call South Carolina and north-central Georgia. The Oconee were a large and linguistically distinctive population, some of whom were strongly influenced by their trading relationships with upcountry British settlers, with whom they engaged in a limited trade in enslaved Africans.

The growing hostility of Indigenous communities contributed to the decline of St. Augustine as a viable or prosperous colonial center. As a result, the security and stability of St. Augustine itself came under threat. With the appointment of a series of new governors—beginning with one Melchor de Navarrete—the strategic need to reestablish a second Fort Mose became an overt security imperative of Spanish authorities.

The formerly enslaved Africans, for their part, had been living in the relative safety of St. Augustine for more than a decade and did not want to leave the protection of the walled town or expose themselves unnecessarily to the hostility of Indigenous communities in conflict with the Spanish colonialists. This, in addition to intensifying pressure being exerted from the north by the expanding British enslavement-farm system and the emerging American white settler independence movement, which was gaining strength with the passage of time.[1] Even the Christianized Natives living in close proximity to St. Augustine sought refuge behind the walls of the town at night.[2] Consequently, many of the freedom seekers who had lived and worked in the relative safety of St. Augustine now resisted the reestablishment of Fort Mose by the colonial administration.

Motivated as much by racism as by military necessity, yet another new governor, Fulgencio Garcia De Solis, ordered the African residents of St. Augustine to rebuild and repopulate Fort Mose on a new site nearby to the original. This decree faced strong resistance from those who would become residents of the new fort, who the frustrated governor said were motivated solely by a "desire to live in complete liberty." The governor paid wages for the work of rebuilding the fort, but punished anyone who resisted the labor. The exact nature of these punishments was not recorded.[3]

When we consider this level of state coercion, it is hard to make a case that the second Fort Mose was as autonomous as the first, even though the first was in existence for only a very short time. This second attempt was more externally controlled and it could be argued that the Africans' resistance to this policy of forced resettlement was a continued manifestation of their desire for freedom, safety, and security. Nevertheless, a second Fort Mose was established and its relationship with St. Augustine was becoming more complicated as the colonial history of Spanish Florida unfolded.

This second fort was part of an expanded defensive network of fortifications to the east and south of St. Augustine and a long defensive line extending to the west. A forest standing between Fort Mose and St. Augustine was felled to increase visibility and a four-foot-high earthen wall extended all the way to the San Sebastián River on the west to defend against land attacks from Indigenous communities who saw their interests as divergent from the creole community in and around St. Augustine.[4]

---

1   Landers, *Black Society in Spanish Florida*, 158–159

2   Landers, *Black Society in Spanish Florida*, 57.

3   Jane Landers, *Gracia Real de Santa Teresa de Mose: A Free Black Town in Spanish Colonial Florida* (St. Augustine: St. Augustine Historical Society, 1992), 28.

4   Landers, *Black Society in Spanish Florida*, 48 and 57.

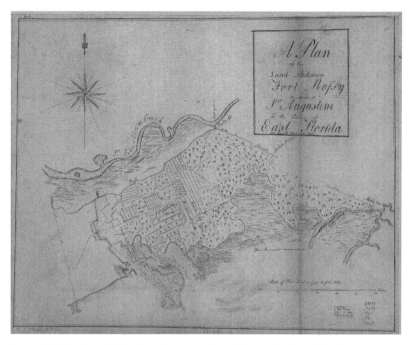

Figure 13. "A plan of the land between Fort Mossy (*sic*) and St. Augustine in the province of East Florida," by Sam Roworth, n.d., 1760s. Note the "Spanish [defensive] line" (right) and the "cleared land" (left).

The second Fort Mose was nevertheless a vital component of this complex of creole settlements, which was developing into an integrated network of interdependent communities from 1752 to 1763. Within this context, there existed a relatively autonomous civil community that maintained a militia, which in turn depended upon the small civil community for at least some of its legitimacy.

Although populations fluctuated, the number of the inhabitants living at Fort Mose is generally acknowledged to have been approximately one hundred people depending upon the year of the count. There was an official census reported by the Spanish colonial government which recorded the population of the second fort at sixty-seven in 1759.[5] The original Mose settlement had also been small, but it grew with the frequent arrival

---

5   Landers, *Black Society in Spanish Florida*, Appendix 5.

of new freedom seekers from the Carolinas. It had been comparatively less integrated into the social fabric of St. Augustine, and had not been directly coerced by Spanish authorities. The first Mose embodied and institutionalized the independently manifested freedom-seeking aspirations of enslaved Africans. All of this is evidence for more autonomy in the daily lives of the people devoid of undue external influences. In short, the first Fort Mose had been more African, more intimate, and more directly democratic.

The second Fort Mose, on the other hand, was largely the product of state coercion. It was more integrated into a creolized colony and was, therefore, subject to the direct influences of the Catholic Church, the creolized Spanish culture, and the Crown. While the resettled population was small, it was made up of people who had become a vital part of the St. Augustine community, even in its precipitous decline. As a result, the second Mose lacked the zeal for autonomy embodied by the first Mose. Such as it was, even this second fort allowed for intimate and consistent social interaction. Inhabitants maintained intimate knowledge of each other as they came and went within the garrison community and between the surrounding villages and St. Augustine itself on a regular basis.

By 1759 more than twenty years had passed since the founding of the first Fort Mose, but this was still a very small and intimate community engaged in the day-to-day activities that allowed it to maintain and sustain a relatively autonomous existence. Some distinguishing demographic features of the second Fort Mose community, according to that year's census, are the following: there were now fifteen adult women and thirty-seven adult men in residence. There were twenty-two households; thirteen of which could be described as nuclear families (i.e., a male adult and a female adult with one or more minor children). There were only two unattached adult women living at the fort. Many of the nine male-only households included men who had wives who were enslaved and even children whose residences were in St. Augustine. There were no single women living as heads of households. A significant proportion of the total population were minor children (seven boys and eight girls).[6]

A priest, appointed by the Church, was responsible for the establishment and maintenance of the small school as well as the local church.

---

6   Landers, *Black Society in Spanish Florida,* Appendix 5.

Several different priests served the second Fort Mose during the period of its existence. As in most parishes, the Church was responsible for important record keeping, including an irregular periodic census and other reports, which often portrayed the priest and his administrative effectiveness in a favorable light. Due to the great deal of coming and going and because many of the inhabitants of the garrison maintained external lives as evidenced by their wives, families, and property in St. Augustine and in the surrounding communities, the census may not have clearly reflected the basic itinerant nature of this community. Even so the community at the fort appeared to be relatively stable.

The final census of Fort Mose was published in 1764 (the year following the mass evacuation of the fort and of St. Augustine itself) and marks a final decline in the community's autonomy. The report lists Commandant Don Geronimo de Hita y Salazar, a member of one of St. Augustine's most elite Spanish families, as the commanding officer of the Mose militia. Chaplain Don Agustin Geronimo Resio is listed as second in command. Interestingly, Capt. Francisco Menendez, now nearly sixty years of age, is recorded as third in command.[7] In an earlier census taken in 1759, neither Commandant Salazar nor the Chaplain Resio are listed as residents. It is not clear if they ever lived in the community. Menendez, however, is listed among the residents in both 1759 and 1764.[8] In any event, the command of the Black militia was clearly no longer in the hands of Black people at Fort Mose on the eve of the Spanish evacuation.

The comparative influence of the Catholic Church from the first iteration of Fort Mose to the second can serve as an indication of a change in the cultural identity of the original freedom seekers. In the earliest days of the first Mose there were no officially freed Africans within the militia and at the second Mose the militia was populated almost exclusively by freed Africans with twenty-one of the most senior residents having been baptized as Catholics within the settlement by 1759. Many of them had lived within St. Augustine and, by then, actually owned land and maintained a life within the evolving creole social hierarchy there. It is not clear if any of the agricultural plots in and around the second Mose

---

7   Landers, *Black Society in Spanish Florida*, Appendix 3.
8   Landers, *Black Society in Spanish Florida*, Appendix 5.

were privately owned. If the precedent established in the first Mose is an indication, these plots would have been property of the Spanish Crown, since most of the inhabitants were themselves still officially enslaved and were not in ownership even of themselves. Residents of Fort Mose would have worked the land as community property, consistent with their own cultural traditions, retained from their lives in Africa.

The plots of land in and around the second Fort Mose were doubtlessly administered, however informally, through the Church. Labor, though free, appeared to be organized much like the plantation task system except that the produce was owned and used by those who worked it. It was worked in some cases individually or in some cases collectively and shared according to a consensus reached by the producers and administered somewhat informally, since there is no official record or map reflecting any pattern of private ownership. Most of the agricultural products of the fort, along with the foods produced by hunting and fishing, were consumed locally. There was, however, some very limited surplus that was traded within the immediate area outside of the wall and within St. Augustine itself.

In the its final years before the evacuation of 1763, many of the Mose residents owned plots within the city of St. Augustine, where meticulous records of private ownership were kept. There is no record of their markets, but it is likely that these were decentralized, irregular, and governed by a system of barter. Most notably absent, though, was the production and shipment of large-scale commercial crops for sale on the world market in any degree comparable to the rice, tobacco or other commodities produced on the enslaved-labor farms of the British settler colonies.

CHAPTER 13
THE EVACUATION OF 1763

The combined population of St. Augustine and Fort Mose was around three thousand individuals at the time of the 1763 Treaty of Paris and the subsequent evacuation to Havana. One quarter of this population were freed Africans.[1] After the evacuation, most of Spanish eastern Florida became open to British colonial settlement. According to the treaty, the Spanish Crown was to regain Havana and the rest of Cuba (which had recently been captured by the British) in exchange for giving up all its claims to Florida. With some assurances of the protection of Spanish private and Church property, the evacuation began in August 1763. Over the next four months there was a steady departure of passengers and cargo.

On 7 August 1763 the last remaining residents of the second Fort Mose settlement, including Captain Francisco Menendez, Lieutenant Antonio Eligio De la Puente, Ensign Francisco Escovedo, along with some forty-eight others, left St. Augustine aboard a ship named the *Nuestra Senora de los Dolores* (Our Lady of Sorrows), bound for Havana and completely integrated with the other evacuees.[2] By January 1764 the last Spanish ship departed from the harbor at St. Augustine. On board were the governor, his complement of bureaucrats, the parish priest, the last residents, and those free Africans who chose exile in Havana. With their departure, the freedom struggle against slavery on the continent of North America now passed to those who would remain in the region to

---

1   Ira Berlin, *Many Thousands Gone* (Cambridge: BelknapPress, 1998), 73–76.
2   Landers, *Black Society in Spanish Florida*, 61.

oppose the rapid expansion of the plantation-owning merchants flooding in from the north to fill the vacuum of colonial power.

As the evacuees made their dutiful and obedient departure, outside of the city walls it was a different story. Other communities, composed of "dozens of Amerindians, runaway slaves, frontiersmen, traders, and 'Crackers' (impoverished whites)," were "not bound by any old or new paper treaty."[3] These remaining self-organized and ethnically diverse eco-communities proliferated throughout the hinterlands and backwoods of Florida, following their own unique patterns of development. These communities continued to mount a challenge to the retention and expansion of the institutionalized enslavement of agricultural labor and the expropriation of Native lands, upon which the newly formed United States was to fight and win its war for independence from the British Crown. Indeed, there were numerous communities springing up throughout Florida that greatly resembled the first Fort Mose.

THE BRITISH EVACUATION

By the end of the U.S. war for independence (which was fought to preserve institutions of human enslavement and to create a new peripheral—but genocidally expansive—state that claimed to be the institutional embodiment of the assertation that "all men are created equal") eastern Florida had become the fourteenth British colony and remained loyal to the British Crown as massive numbers of loyalists evacuated the Carolinas, Virginia, Georgia, and other pockets of loyalism, escaping to the south to seek protection of their persons and of their enslaved property.

In the aftermath of their military victory against the British Empire (which was also faced with a growing abolitionist movement), the thirteen former colonies began to form a more centralized political and economic union with the creation of a new Constitution in 1787, which enshrined the permanent lifetime enslavement of African laborers. Africans (both enslaved and free), Indigenous peoples, and propertyless white classes represented such an overwhelming disenfranchised, exploited, and oppressed majority that any claim to a popular "democracy" in the United States was ludicrous from the moment of its conception.

---

3   James W. Raab, *Spain, Britain and the American Revolution in Florida, 1763-1783*, (Jefferson: McFarland & Company), 18.

As of 20 April 1783, at the conclusion of the military phase of the War of American Independence, an official census of British loyalist refugees coming from the other colonies to eastern Florida were the following: "6,090 whites, 11,285 negros, totaling some 17,285 people."[4] It is unclear from these numbers which Negros were enslaved and which were free. In fact, it was not altogether clear who were Negros and who were not. That is a lingering problem with any census based on race or any other fleeting arbitrary social category, especially during the period of our present study.

But there existed and even greater flaw with this census count. Native people—or more specifically, members of diverse eco-communities who owed no allegiance to the imperial crown of Britain, the new emerging American racist state, or the rapidly withering Spanish colonial state—went uncounted. They existed in significant numbers, but their proportional population in the region is difficult to assess since they did not fall within the scope of the census.

During this twenty-year period of the occupation of eastern Florida by the British (1763–1783), tens of thousands of defeated loyalists were engaged in a mad scramble to maintain their property in the form of human capital (enslaved people) and all manner of proof of ownership over this property in the form of currency and other certificates. They were attempting to salvage as much as they could and to relocate their families and fortunes in the face of the rapid expansion of the American settlers' enslavement farm system, supported by an emerging manufacturing, commercial, and financial sector in the urbanizing northeast of the new United States.

Native communities, enslaved populations, and landless whites were not party to the ongoing treaty negotiations of the period. After the 1783 Treaty of Paris (not to be confused with the earlier 1763 Treaty of Paris), which officially ended the conflict between the British and Americans, these marginalized communities began to disappear into the swamps and backwoods across the St. Johns River.[5] Doubtless they continued to hope that whatever colonial power gained control over eastern Florida, they would honor earlier treaties that had affirmed Indigenous community

---

4   Wilbur H. Siebert, *Loyalists in East Florida, 1774-1784*, Vol. 1 (Boston: Gregg Press, 1929), 131.

5   Raab, *Spain, Britain and the American Revolution in Florida, 1763-1783*, 158.

control of the land on the western side of the river. It was a reasonable but short-lived expectation.

Prior to the 1783 Treaty of Paris, a series of preliminary peace treaties were signed by the representatives of the United States and Great Britain providing for the evacuation of loyalists from Savannah on 11 July 1782 and from Charleston by December of that same year. These evacuees were transported to East Florida. It is estimated that at least one hundred thousand loyalists left the thirteen colonies during the war to maintain slavery, which many still refer to as the "American revolution."[6] Many of them found themselves in Florida initially and from there they were transported to other regions of the British empire or back to Britain itself.[7]

These British Loyalists and their defeated allies, a large number of enslaved and freed Africans among them, were widely scattered throughout the territories of the British Empire. They went to places like Abaco and many of the other islands of the present-day Bahama archipelago. Others landed in Jamaica or Dominica. Some went north to Nova Scotia and other parts of Canada. Still others reached as far as South America while some daringly remained within the confines of what was becoming the United States. Everywhere they were attempting, in one way or another, to escape the monster slave state that was enveloping them.

Those who stayed formed communities in the hinterlands and remote places where the authority of alien governments and states could not interfere with the establishment of their own intimately democratic authority. Many even set up secret autonomous social formations just outside the boundaries of the enslaved-labor farms where so many Africans were held in bondage. Others sought refuge deep in remote natural spaces where they could live in peace.

The largest recorded of these ethnically diverse maroon communities was a settlement called Angola, which was established in 1812 at a freshwater mineral spring near the Manatee River, south of Tampa Bay, on Florida's western coast. Angola was home to over seven hundred

6   See Gerald Horne, *The Counter-Revolution of 1776: Slave Resistance and the Origins of the United States of America* (New York: New York University Press, 2014) for an affirmation of this proposition.

7   Raab, *Spain, Britain and the American Revolution in Florida, 1763-1783*, 170.

freedom-seeking people thriving on the outskirts of the U.S. and Spanish empires. The community was attacked and destroyed by the U.S. military when Florida became a U.S. territory in 1821. Many of the community's inhabitants fled to Andros Island in the Bahamas.[8]

THE RETURN OF THE SPANISH, U.S. ANNEXATION, AND THE SEMINOLE WARS

The British crown, weakened by a long and failed struggle to maintain the thirteen colonies and faced with intensifying hostility in northern East Florida from a new wave of aggressive slave-owning settlers continued to negotiate a series of treaties with what was becoming the new United States of America. These negotiations were part of a broader set of compromises that resulted in a series of protocols between the competing European colonial powers with shifting interests in the Western Hemisphere. Among many other provisions, the 1783 Treaty of Paris allowed the Spanish to return to Florida. The British Loyalists evacuated and relinquished all claims to the land, but after Spain's twenty-year absence Florida had become a very different place.

Upon their return, Spanish authorities encountered a large ethnically and racially diverse backwoods and swamp-dwelling population living in a network of small eco-communities. These were the people that they left behind some twenty years before: the people who owed no loyalty to any state or empire. They were more numerous, more autonomous, more integrated with their natural surroundings, more rebellious, more socially "developed." This diverse, backwoods, swamp population who lived their lives in resistance to the institutions of slavery were called "*cimarrons*" by the Spanish, meaning "renegades" or "runaways." Through living usage by distinctive interacting cultural currents over time, these same people eventually came to be known as the "Seminoles." The self-organized, autonomous, and intimately democratic Seminole communities had formed an institutional basis for freedom-seeking people in the region.

---

8   The present-day city of Bradenton, Florida now stands on the site of the former Angola maroon community. Rosalyn Howard, "Looking for Angola: An Archaeological and Ethnohistorical Search for a Nineteenth Century Florida Maroon Community and its Caribbean Connections," *The Florida Historical Quarterly*, Vol. 92, No. 1 (Summer 2013), 32–68. (A.Z.)

They lived in ecological symbiosis with natural spaces. They fought the expansionistic efforts of the marauding American slavery system that was reducing people to property and robbing others of life, destroying their social institutions and knowledge systems by forcefully separating them from their means of collective social and ecological support. They also created trading cooperatives and mutual defense confederations that fought a protracted war of resistance to the ongoing Indigenous genocide.

This confluence of the struggle against African enslavement and the struggle against Indigenous genocide later came to a head in the so-called "Seminole Wars" (1817–1818, 1835–1842, and 1855–1858), which occurred during and after the aggressive U.S. annexation of Florida in the first half of the nineteenth century. These were the longest and bloodiest of the so-called "American Indian Wars."

After repeated "Indian Removal Acts" by the United States, many Seminoles were removed to Oklahoma but still others moved deeper south into the Everglades, seeking a more autonomous and intimately democratic way of life. In this ongoing resistance to the diabolical and cannibalistic expansionism of the U.S. slave state, we find a continuation of the Florida maroons' freedom-seeking aspirations and the best impulses of Fort Mose's legacy as the struggle continues.

Part Three: Discussion

RE-LEARNING THE PAST TO RE-IMAGINE THE FUTURE

Modibo Kadalie in conversation with Andrew Zonneveld

On 10 April 2021, Modibo Kadalie and Andrew Zonneveld met over a video call to further reflect on the histories of the Great Dismal Swamp and Fort Mose as they relate to the development of an intimate and directly democratic politics. The conversation focused especially on the relevance of these histories to present-day and future radical social movements and began with Dr. Kadalie clarifying the meaning of intimate direct democracy in practice.

Andrew Zonneveld: First, can you speak more about the concept of intimate direct democracy? How does social intimacy relate to direct democracy? How does the desire for an intimately democratic life animate the histories that you've discussed in this book?

Modibo Kadalie: Intimate direct democracy is what many Indigenous peoples in the Americas were already practicing at the time of European invasion. We need to learn from it. It's the kind of life in which people can sit down, talk with one another, and reach some kind of consensus about how they want to live, how they want to relate to their immediate environment, and how they want to structure their institutions and carry on their history. The most fundamental basis of direct democracy is its intimacy. In order for direct democracy to exist there must be an intimate knowledge of the people involved, both individually and collectively. Direct democracy can not occur among people who are anonymous with respect to one another. The motivation and reputation of everyone must be known to all.[1]

This book offers two historical examples that were not really similar (Fort Mose was a settlement built by a group of people while the Great Dismal Swamp was a natural place) and uses them to explore Indigenous directly democratic traditions emanating from North America and Africa. Through these examples, we come to understand a radically different history of democracy than we have been taught.

What we find missing in the great propaganda efforts that masquerade as histories of the United States is the fact that the U.S. has never created any form of democracy. We sometimes hear the U.S. being referred to as a "great experiment in democracy," but in this book I wanted to show that the U.S. actually destroyed—exterminated—real democratic institutions at every turn. More than that, they also decimated the land itself. The founding of the United States was, in fact, a great ecological and social catastrophe.

We see it on the land and water from the Great Dismal Swamp to the north all the way south to Fort Mose and beyond to southern Florida. Some people call it development, but to me, it's all messed up. There are all kinds of industry polluting the land, rivers, and ocean, especially the pulp and paper mills we see up and down the coast. So, I wanted to show that *this* has been the meaning of the United States from its very beginning. It was never a "great experiment in democracy." It wasn't in the beginning and it's certainly not now.

Remember, too, that Benjamin Franklin, who was one of the great U.S. ideologues, lived in Pennsylvania, right in the middle of what was

---

1 This is why the anonymity of the internet and social media, in the present period, places severe limitations on its directly democratic potential. Present and future communications technologies must be consciously and intentionally developed to facilitate the most intimate accountability and unity of propose, as well as mutual support and cooperation. The toxic anonymity of the internet has to be reduced in order to accomplish meaningful respect and trust. This effort, however, cannot be accomplished through the authority of states and corporate powers. In order for cultures of accountability and democracy to thrive on the internet, the technology must be almost entirely reimagined and redeveloped as a commons for which all of us are equally responsible. (M.K.)

the Haudenosaunee Confederacy. Franklin used the Haudenosaunee as a model during the Albany Congress while he was advocating a confederation of the English colonies. The Haudenosaunee Confederacy, though it may not have been directly democratic, it was a republican form of government. They are largely not given credit for their influence. You can see their influence as the U.S. Constitution was being drafted in 1787. But the funny thing about that Constitutional Convention is you see a lot of talk about trade. They are very concerned about free trade. To them, freedom never meant freedom of people. It meant freedom to make money. So, whenever we hear these politicians today talking about "freedom, justice, and equality for all," I just say: "Yeah, yeah. We know what you're really talking about."

Andrew: Right. And in the midst of all of this violence and colonization of what became the emerging U.S. empire, there were actual examples of direct democracy happening on the peripheries—at places like the Great Dismal Swamp and Fort Mose. The people in those places lived their lives in resistance to the slavery and colonialism that defined the European presence in North America.

You mentioned in Part Two of this book that there existed many other such directly democratic communities of refuge and resistance, especially in Florida. One of the most remarkable of these sites existed near present-day Bradenton and is remembered by the name Angola, Florida. This site has only recently been the subject of serious archeological study and there is very little written about it. Compared to Fort Mose, however, it was a very large community of about seven hundred people who lived spread-out around the Manatee mineral spring.

As you know, I visited the site earlier this year. During my trip, I learned that there were also once mounds on the bank of the Manatee River. They predate the founding of the Angola community in 1812 and have since been destroyed, but they were intact when maroons lived in the area. As we know, mound-building cultures feature prominently in your historical contextualization of Fort Mose. Having worked with you on this book, I was really struck by how the intersecting histories that you describe were all right there under my feet in the small city of Bradenton.

According to the archeological record, these local mounds may not have been in use at the same time as the Angola community was established, but we know that the mounds were there, and that Indigenous people were there, and the folks who lived at the Angola site had meaningful day-to-day relationships with Indigenous people.

Communities like these were eventually besieged by U.S. raids and the survivors were forced to flee. Some refugees from the Angola site fled to Andros in the Bahamas and others joined with local Indigenous communities.

Archeological research at this site has largely been a community effort led by Black citizens of Bradenton. They have, of course, sought the involvement of some professional researchers, but the major impetus for the excavation of the Angola site was undertaken by ordinary Black citizens who were not necessarily affiliated with any university but whose ancestors had themselves once sought freedom and built their community in this place.

Modibo: What is so interesting is that it's really hard to tell who was Native and who was African in a site like that one. Everyone lived together. They were all freedom-seeking people. There were probably some white people there too. I bet some of them even had blue eyes. [*laughs*]

Andrew: Could be! [*laughs*] It seems to me, though, that sites like these are constantly being uncovered as historians and archeologists continue to investigate histories like these. Can you comment on the future of these studies? I'm especially interested in your evaluation of the role of community science in these endeavors.

Modibo: Well, when the people from the universities start coming in there to study this shit, you gotta watch 'em! Be careful with that. Keep an eye on these people and make sure they don't misinterpret everything. I think that new technologies have allowed ordinary people to study these things on our own authority. And when we learn this history, we can see that it's really *our* story. It is *us*.

In order to have a vision of the future the first thing we must do is ask ourselves: "Is *this* it? Is this how our story is going to go? Is this how the world is going to be, with nation-states, governments, and corporations centralizing all of the wealth and authority?" When we decide that we don't want *that* to be the case, we have to reimagine the future. In order to do that well, we have to understand the past and our evolving role as living social creatures sharing this planet with the rest of the natural world.

So, the archeological effort being made at the Angola site in Bradenton is not merely an academic exercise. It's an example of humanity trying to understand where we came from and, in so doing, trying to understand how we want to live on this planet and share it with each other and with other living things.

I'm really impressed with younger people. They are convinced that the nation-state is not offering them a future. Newer generations of researchers are now beginning to look for evidence of community and collectivity. In the past, people studying some archeological site would be asking "Where did the privileged people live? Where did the priest live? If there's a mound, I guess he must have lived at the top!" [*laughs*] But once these new technologies are taken up by ordinary people who are studying our real collective past and creating a new vision for the future, they'll do a much better job than any professional academics ever have. That doesn't only apply to exploring human sites, but, equally, to the exploration of nature—whether that's on land, in the ocean, or somewhere else.

The story is clear to us now. Humans typically don't want anything to do with hierarchical societies or the oppressive institutions that these societies create. Those structures and ideas are imposed upon us by a few people who want power, but we can always find ways to escape it. Meaningful human equality can never be granted to anyone by a government. That's something all of us must assert for ourselves. And that's what these community archeological efforts are doing. They are asserting their community's place in history and its contribution to the human tradition of intimate direct democracy. And that's what our effort with this book has been, too.

Andrew: Wow, yes. That was very well said. Let's circle back later to this idea of critical historiography as political practice, but before we take that any further, I'm curious how you might relate the histories of the Great

Dismal Swamp and Fort Mose to the histories of the Gullah Geechee. Where do they enter the story that you've outlined in this book?

Modibo: The Yamasee were a multi-ethnic group of people. When they lost the Yamasee War—which was essentially an effort by large numbers of Indigenous peoples and African maroons fighting to chase the English out of what is now South Carolina—alliances began to weaken, and many people fled south. There, they assimilated with local Native peoples and a growing population of trafficked and enslaved African laborers. This creolized culture, made up of a central core of Africans recently imported from the upper Guinea rice coast, became what we know today as the Gullahs of the South Carolina coast and the Geechees of the Georgia coast.

Most of the people trafficked to this region came from Western Africa who held communal scientific and agricultural knowledge of rice cultivation. They had been enslaved by the British and trafficked in huge numbers to North America, where they were forced to do the same work that they had once done for the benefit of their own communities, only now they were doing it under threat of horrific violence for the profit of European colonizers.

Ecologically speaking, however, they were much more at home than the British. When you look at maps of South Carolina and the Guinea Coast, they are almost like mirror images. The rivers, tides, plant and animal life, are all very similar. So, Gullah-Geechee people brought their indigenous knowledge from Africa to the South Carolina (and eventually Georgia) coasts. They understood the ecosystems here. As maroons, they went deeper into the swamps and woods, where they maintained a certain amount of cultural homogeneity and continuity with Africa, which continued after the U.S. Civil War into the present day. That's where some stereotypes come from: a Geechee is a person who likes rice, eats fish, and who don't take no shit from nobody. He's shorter in stature and very dark. And he talks funny (because of his creole dialect).

The linguistic variable is important. Linguistics are an important part of history and archeology. In this book, I discuss that with respect to the Tuscarora and their relationship to the Haudenosaunee. Nowadays, technology has made all of this easier to study because we can record spoken language with devices we carry in our pockets every day. Added to that are the communications technologies of the internet and the use of lasers and RADAR to map archeological sites. I think a lot of new things are going to be uncovered that reframe how we understand the past. Here on the coast, there are people who use laser technology to study grave sites of enslaved people. They find grave sites everywhere, man. All of this new technology can be used to help gather the real history of this region. We are going to see a shift for sure. You and I are part of it, to tell you the truth. And I'm glad to be a part of it.

Andrew: Me too. I was recently watching this old taped episode of *60 Minutes* from 1983 when Mike Wallace was reporting the story of Harris Neck [a Geechee community that was forcibly displaced in the 1940s]. In the video, Rev. Edgar Timmons Jr. and other folks were out at the Gould Cemetery clearing brush. Apparently, some white landowners had let their cattle graze and trample across the cemetery. I had no idea that the cemetery had once been so overgrown and so mistreated. I couldn't help but wonder how many other Black cemeteries in the area had been destroyed by white folks in the area.

Modibo: That's why it's so important for ordinary people to get familiar with these new technologies. If we can learn to use these laser tools, maybe we can go out in the woods and find our great-great grandparents.

Andrew: Do you have any worries or concerns about the increasing academic interest in Gullah-Geechee culture?

Modibo: My worry is that these historians and archeologists will come here looking for stories about great leaders and charismatic individuals, as opposed to looking at the democratic social organization of the area. They'll be looking to see who owned the most land, or which preacher had the biggest church, instead of studying how people lived and made decisions within their community.

Look at the Black Baptist church down here, for example. In some ways, it's a very democratic institution. It's decentralized. Originally, there were no Bishops. And really no hierarchy. The churches were not owned by individual preachers and the preachers are recallable. There are other similar churches that might get founded with entrepreneurial intentions—and maybe some white folks come along and give them some money—but those are an anti-democratic reaction to the democracy in the original Black Baptist churches. In the church that I grew up in, we voted every year on whether or not to keep the preacher. Even the little kids voted. This is a fundamental part of Geechee culture down here on the coast. It's slowly being destroyed, like everything else down here, but there are some lingering traditions that people hold onto.

Andrew: Wow, I didn't realize that! On the topic of democratic traditions, I wanted to ask you another question. Although the title of this book is *Intimate Direct Democracy*, it is not a how-to guide for creating radically democratic or egalitarian communities. Instead, it's a historiographic exploration of how we can use direct democracy as a critical lens for better understanding history itself. Why do you take this approach, as opposed to more prescriptive approaches to writing about political theory?

Modibo: Well, if we believe in direct democracy that means that we must believe that ordinary people can create institutions to liberate themselves and drive history forward. So, to get those ideas across, we can't just start telling people what to do and how to do it. It doesn't work that way (unless, of course, you are offering your own point of view in a specific context to solve a specific problem). So, what I'm attempting to do with this book is to help people to look at our own history. Hopefully we will see that we have been lied to about our history and that could shift the way we understand the world and inform how we want to embrace and contribute to this rich historical legacy.

It is understandable but unfortunate that almost all of history has been written from an elitist perspective. It's very carefully constructed. The purpose of writing history in that way is partly to ensure that anyone who comes forward to challenge the status quo must have all of the answers to all of the questions facing their society. If you don't have an answer for everything, then you're looked at as incompetent. But human knowledge doesn't really unfold in that way. Human knowledge unfolds through people working together and finding their answers collaboratively. That's what science is: socially derived answers to a given problem. But if you've got people who allegedly know all the answers, they will think of themselves as more important than all of the other people who they think don't know anything.

Critical historiography should allow us to see ourselves in our most democratic essence, through self-examination of our histories so that we can self-manage our societies. It's a very simple concept, but it's very strongly opposed in a society that is so rigid, with such powerful instruments of propaganda. It's hard to break through it, but we *are* breaking through. I can see it. I can see that people are beginning to grasp it. I think that's because elitist politics have failed everyone so badly in the past. The prevailing top-down worldview of history and everything else has led to some catastrophic consequences and now people are seeking a way out of this—but that's not to say that anyone will lead them! They will lead themselves.

Andrew: We have talked a lot about historians' relationships to freedom struggles, but what about activists' and organizers' relationship to history? How can we understand and articulate critical historiography itself as a political project, and why is it so important for people involved in freedom struggles today to become familiar with an anti-hierarchical view of history?

Modibo: If we look at history closely, we will find that social movements really are *social* movements. Some are more hierarchical than others, but those that are in their most directly democratic form tend to be the most successful, especially when they erupt spontaneously. Then later, of course, the state creeps in and chops them up, channeling energies here and there, but when it first erupts it is a pure expression of social will by a collective of oppressed people.

Now, in order for us to best understand what we are doing while we are in social motion, we need to know what our predecessors have done in similar situations. We need history as a guide, but it can't be a guide to hierarchical organization because our history and our experience has already shown that's a dead end to more oppression. So, if history is going to be relevant to social movements, it must be understood as a guide to non-hierarchical, democratic organization. Luckily, if we look at the long arc of human social history, that's exactly how our most fulfilling and liberating institutions have been organized. When we learn this history and then turn to see the exploitation, pollution, wars, and other deadly conflicts we have in our societies now, this lifestyle will seem inhuman to us and we should want to do something to change it. An anti-war movement, for example, is the most human kind of movement that we can have because it's a movement against the most inhuman of activities.

If a movement is going to move forward, we have to understand that what we are doing is not new. People have fought in the struggle for freedom many times in the past and intimate direct democracy is the way that they have moved forward. There are, of course, some people who haven't moved at all. They will try to take the movement in another direction, and they will have to be called out and exposed, especially in our study of history.

History has to be a politically conscious and very intentional project, and a social movement should have people willing to do research, to dig down deep into this stuff and provide the movement with examples of direct democracy in action. That's how we crystalize a vision for the future: by establishing a continuity from the rich democratic past toward a more enriching and much broader directly democratic future.

Andrew: There have been many recent contestations over public history, especially movements aimed at removing Confederate statues and other racist monuments. Often, the activists involved in these struggles are very young. Here in Decatur, [Georgia] where I live, a group of high school students successfully campaigned to have a Confederate monument removed from the public square. You have also personally been involved in some public history projects, like the preservation of the Historic Baptismal Trail in Riceboro.[2] Do you see involvement in public history projects as an aspect of activism?

---

2   From 2000 until 2009, Modibo was involved in a successful effort to preserve the site of a traditional Gullah-Geechee baptismal pool in Riceoboro, Georgia. The site is now maintained by the city, protected from destructive industrial development, and commemorated by a historical walking trail that includes historical markers and descriptions of local ecology. (A.Z.)

Modibo: Yeah, I do. We have to be careful with the younger activists, though. We have to challenge them to stand up for themselves without us throttling their efforts. They need to know that their demands are justified regardless of what any law says, because the laws were written by people who do not have our interests at heart. Slavery was the law of the land at one time, after all.

When young people start moving, it's a beautiful thing. Our role is to stop the state from creeping in. When the state creepers come around that's when the young folks need us the most. [*laughs*]

Andrew: So, is that your advice to younger generations involved in these struggles: "watch out for politicians?"

Modibo: Watch out for the politicians, for the state creep, and make sure you do your research and understand your research perspective clearly. In science, we use observation to substantiate our assertions. Sometimes we're right, sometimes we're not. There are some people who can't give up on their assertions, oh my goodness. The world tells them one thing and they will deny their eyes and their ears refusing to believe it. That's really a danger in society, when people deny what's going on. There is a propaganda machine out there with unbelievable power. Young people are subject to it. We're all subject to it. It informs how we think about everything in the world, including our own history. We need to be aware of it and develop our ability to examine the world on our own authority.

Religion is a tricky thing too. Earlier, we were talking about the Baptist church as a quasi-democratic institution. I wasn't talking about their system of beliefs. A cosmology can be a dangerous thing. At least with science, you can check and verify people's cosmological assertions.

We must learn to think more critically. After George Floyd was murdered by the Minneapolis police, there were some people who almost portrayed Mr. Floyd as a modern hero—and I guess that's fine—but it's more important to get people to examine the institutions behind Mr. Floyd's murder. It's not about anything that Mr. Floyd or his family did on their own, but his death took place at a certain time and in a certain context. That's what inspires mass motion. It's important to understand race and class, too. Identity politics can be important but limiting and we should be very aware of those limitations. After all, many of the people taking action at the protests and uprisings last summer in Minneapolis, and all over the world, were white. I think it's important to find allies where we can, not just allies who look like us.

Above all, critical historiography is the most important thing. We have to be able to look critically at our own perspectives on history, because they reflect how we understand the world around us. We must proceed from the point of view that hierarchy is dangerous and that, if continued, it will destroy us all. It will wipe away all life from this planet. So, we must stop it. The way we stop it is by dismantling the nation-state and dismantling these corporations through our own directly democratic efforts. To do that, we must acknowledge and affirm the social upheavals that create directly democratic social institutions and relations, support and build upon them the intimate, horizontal, and democratic communities that spring forth from the bottom of society.

Andrew: I know that you and Rev. Zack Lyde have recently been outspoken against mineral extraction in the areas around the Okefenokee Swamp. In Part One of your book, you describe swamp land as an almost inherently anti-capitalist space. Can you talk a little more about this?

Modibo: What I wanted to show in Part One is that the Great Dismal Swamp was an impediment to the colonial agricultural expansion of tobacco. I mean, you can't grow tobacco in a swamp. You can grow rice in a swamp, though. And that's why Charleston is sometimes called Rice City. I'm from Riceboro, (Georgia) but Charleston is really Rice City.

I also tried to show the impact of certain agricultural commodities coming from the English colonies. The Spanish were not interested in agriculture at all. They were more concerned with extracting gold. The English, however, were interested in agricultural settlement and eventually this became a for-profit enterprise. At first, they used indentured labor, but when they decided that they needed a more ecologically and agriculturally knowledgeable labor force, they started enslaving Africans.

We also have to keep in mind the *Greater* Dismal Swamps: the whole area around the Pamlico Sound is a swamp; the entire southeastern shoreline, spanning south from the Greater Dismal Swamps all the way down to the Everglades, is, to a great extent, swamp land. Remember, the Everglades back in the seventeenth and eighteenth centuries were not the same Everglades that we see now. The Everglades used to extend all the way up to Lake Okeechobee, especially on the western side. At one time, the general area of swamp land could have extended as far up as the Angola site that you mentioned earlier. It was all one big ecosystem, but capitalist expansion and pollution have reduced the Everglades to less than half of its original size.

Andrew: Yeah, that's true. And Florida is now dealing with the fallout of the Everglades' destruction. Wetlands are necessary to provide clean fresh water and protect communities from the effects of hurricanes, as they help to improve water quality and reduce flooding. As wetlands disappear, the effects of hurricanes and water pollution become increasingly severe and that's exactly what's happening in Florida now. The ecological crisis of the wetlands' disappearance is also simultaneously a social crisis because poorer communities are disproportionately hurt by storm damage and water pollution; and all of this ecological destruction was made possible by historical social crises like colonialist land theft, genocide, enslavement, and the continued exploitation of labor.

Modibo: Yes. And let's not forget that the Great Dismal Swamp itself is now only about one tenth of its original size. So, when we visit these swamps and wetlands, we have to not only see the area for what it is, but also for what it was. Just look at the Crystal River area on the Gulf Coast of Florida. It's hard to look at that area now, with all the condos, hotels, billboards, and big houses.

Andrew: Yeah, it's so overdeveloped there. It's terrible. Crystal River, as you know, is a seasonal home to large numbers of manatees. Only one small area around the natural spring has been preserved for their use. All of the surrounding land has been taken over by residential suburban sprawl and there is very heavy boat traffic. I visited there last year to kayak with the manatees and, at your recommendation, I took the opportunity to see the nearby mound site at Crystal River Archeological State Park, a site that was used for burials and ceremonies by Indigenous peoples for almost two thousand continuous years. The juxtaposition of massive suburban sprawl with remnants of the area's pre-colonial ecology and human history was striking.

Modibo: Yeah, it's hard to imagine what it once was. That area could have once been considered to be part of the Everglades ecosystem, broadly speaking. And by the way, the only reason that there is any conservation of the Everglades at all is because the Seminoles work so hard to keep so-called development out of there. The Great Dismal Swamp is that way, too, with the Tuscarora people, who, like the Seminoles, are also very racially and ethnically mixed.

You know, when we first look at this history it's sometimes hard to see through the fog of Jim Crow and slavery to get a clear vision of what was really going on underneath it all. That's what's most interesting about these Confederate monuments: most of them weren't even constructed until this past century, during the era of Jim Crow. They were built to somehow justify Jim Crow. So, when the young people of today discovered that, they said, "Well you took down all the 'For Coloreds' signs, so you better take down these monuments, because they're doing the same thing and they're from the same period." I think that realization helps younger people to look past that era and see further back into history, which can then help them to look forward to a different future.

Andrew: Yeah, and when they look even further back into the past, we can start knocking down all kinds of monuments!

Modibo: [*Laughing*] And then all we have to do is sit back! They will do it more effectively than we ever could.

Andrew: I saw that a bunch of people were arrested last summer in Miami because they tried to destroy a Cristopher Columbus monument. I was very impressed by their effort, but now Florida is considering a law in which attacking a statue has become a felony. It's a whole mess, but it's interesting to see the state's response to recent contestations over public history, which has become a real battlefield this year. Before we end our discussion, though, is there anything else you want to share about this project? Any final thoughts?

Modibo: You know, sometimes people might look at us and say all we do is sit on our asses writing. That shouldn't matter to us. When I think back on my experiences in the Black Power struggle, it seems to me that part of the reason our movement was so susceptible to state creep is because it wasn't rooted in an understanding of our own history. The fundamental flawed assumption of the Civil Rights and Black Power movement of the sixties and seventies was and is that the governments of various nation states could move history forward. It was commonly assumed that liberation could take place by reforming an existing government or by taking over and creating a new government. Our struggle was limited to and contained within the parameters of the nation state. The obvious reformers saw themselves as changing certain critical policies within the state. The "revolutionaries" wanted to seize state power. Various charismatic leaders were able to articulate variations of these basic themes. In this way they were attempting to take—and are still trying to take—the movement in all sorts of different directions, all leading us right back to the state in one form or another.

This is still the most dangerous limitation placed upon our social movements. These people are still being interviewed, by the way. Their books are in all the libraries. So, it's hard to counter the narratives that they have established. There are people who are still saying that there is no tradition of direct democracy among Black people. Or that Black people are looking for a messiah. And, of course, when these charismatic and high-profile people get killed, that's just another part of the state's demoralization of our social movement. So, it's better not to have the high-profile people in the first place. And our work here can help our movements to become better rooted in our own directly democratic past and to look beyond the narrow politics of charismatic individuals.

Andrew: I think a strength of our recent work, especially in our public events together, has been our clarity on this idea. In every public talk you've had, there is someone who says, "I hear what you're saying about this direct democracy stuff, but what do we *do*?" And in our responses,

I think that you and I have been successful at dispelling the idea that intellectual work and activism are somehow separate. Part of what we "do," is doing history: re-learning and re-explaining the struggles that have already happened so that the right ideas are in the right place at the right time when those situations emerge again. Critical research is a very important aspect of effective activism and organizing, but some people have a hard time wrapping their brains around that idea.

Modibo: Most of the time when people ask, "What should I do?" they're really asking "What organization should I join? What leader do I follow?" So, we must always try to debunk that. We should say that if you find yourself in a movement that has formed around an obviously dominant leader, you might as well go the hell home. That movement is a dead end. But if you have people who are organized around an issue or idea and they are able to sit down and listen to one another and develop a strategy, then you're on the right track. I can't find those people for you. You have to learn to look for them, because those are the people who are making history.

REFERENCES

American University. "Freedom in the Swamp: Unearthing the secret history of the Great Dismal Swamp." *ScienceDaily*. www.sciencedaily.com/releases/2011/05/110516075940.htm.

Berlin, Ira. *Many Thousands Gone.* Cambridge: Belkanp Press, 1998.

Blakemore, Erin. "Amazon Jungle Once Home to Millions More Than Previously Thought." *National Geographic*, 27 March 2018. https://www.nationalgeographic.com/history/article/amazon-jungle-ancient-population-satellite-computer-model.

Campbell, Mavis C. *The Maroons of Jamaica, 1655–1796.* Trenton: Africa World Press, 1990.

Carney, Judith. *Black Rice: The African Origins of Rice Cultivation in the Americas.* Cambridge: Harvard University Press, 2001.

Collins, James M. *The Archaeology of the Cahokia Mounds.* Springfield: Preservation Agency, 1990.

Bookchin, Murray. *The Ecology of Freedom: The Emergence and Dissolution of Hierarchy.* Oakland: AK Press, 2005.

Deagan, Kathleen A., ed. *Spanish St. Augustine: The Archeology of a Creole Community.* New York: Academic Press, 1983.

Roxanne Dunbar-Ortiz, Roxanne. *An Indigenous Peoples' History of the United States.* Boston: Beacon Press, 2014.

Elbein, Asher. "What Doomed a Sprawling City Near St. Louis 1,000 Years Ago?" *The New York Times.* 24 April 2021.

Frank, Andrew. "Creek Indian Leaders." *New Georgia Encyclopedia*. 25 August 2020. https://www.georgiaencyclopedia.org/articles/history-archaeology/creek-indian-leaders.

Gannon, Megan. "The First US City Was Full of Immigrants," *Live Science*. 6 March 2014. https://www.livescience.com/43896-cahokia-ancient-city-immigrants.html

Graeber, David, and David Wengrow. *The Dawn of Everything: A New History of Humanity*. New York: Farrar, Straus and Giroux, 2021.

Fortune, Margo. "Position of three sites of African maroonage in North America—the Great Dismal Swamp, Fort Mose, and Florida's Angola community—in relation to major European colonial centers." Map. 1 January 2021.

Hall, Joseph. "The Great Indian Slave Caper." Review *The Indian Slave Trade: The Rise of the English Empire in the American South, 1670-1717*, by of Alan Gallay. *Commonplace*, Vol. 3, No. 1. October 2002.

Horne, Gerald. *The Counter-Revolution of 1776: Slave Resistance and the Origins of the United States of America*. New York: New York University Press, 2014.

Howard, Rosalyn. "Looking for Angola: An Archaeological and Ethnohistorical Search for a Nineteenth Century Florida Maroon Community and its Caribbean Connections." *The Florida Historical Quarterly*, Vol. 92, No. 1. Summer 2013.

Inomata, Takeshi, D. Triadan, V.A. Vázquez López, et al. "Monumental architecture at Aguada Fénix and the rise of Maya civilization," *Nature* 582. 3 June 2020.

James, C.L.R. *The Black Jacobins: Toussaint L'Ouverture and the San Domingo Revolution*. New York: Random House, 1963.

Junger, Sebastian. *Tribe: On Homecoming and Belonging*. New York: Twelve Press, 2016.

Kadalie, Modibo. *The Independent African American Labor Movement in the Formation of the American State and the Consolidation of American Capitalist Class Power*. Ph.D. Dissertation. Atlanta: Atlanta University, 1989.

Kadalie, Modibo, and Matthew Quest. Voices of Labor Oral History Project, Southern Labor Archives. Special Collections and Archives, Georgia State University. 12 November 2010.

Kadalie, Modibo. *Pan-African Social Ecology: Speeches, Conversations, and Essays.* Atlanta: On Our Own Authority!, 2019.

Kulikoof, Allan. *Tobacco and Slaves: The Development of Southern Cultures in the Chesapeake, 1680–1800.* Chapel Hill: University of North Carolina Press, 1986.

Kupperman, Karen Ordahl. *Roanoke: The Abandoned Colony.* Lanham: Rowman and Littlefield, 1984.

Landers, Jane. *Black Society in Spanish Florida.* Urbana: University of Illinois Press: 1999.

Landers, Jane. *Gracia Real de Santa Teresa de Mose: A Free Black Town in Spanish Colonial Florida.* St. Augustine: St. Augustine Historical Society, 1992.

Landry, Clay J. "Who Drained the Everglades," *Property and Environment Research Center.* Vol. 20, No. 1. Spring 2002.

Lanning, John Tate, and Willis Physioc. "Map of Spanish Missions in Georgia." *The Spanish Missions of Georgia.* Chapel Hill: University of North Carolina Press, 1935. Map.

Lodge, John, and J. Bew. "Plan of the Town and Harbor of St. Augustin, in East Florida, 1783." *Political Magazine.* London: William Child, 1783. Map.

Mark, Joshua J. "Anglo-Powhatan Wars." *World History Encyclopedia.* 25 February 2021. https://www.worldhistory.org/Anglo-Powhatan_Wars.

Mbah, Sam. *African Anarchism: The History of a Movement.* Tuscon: See Sharp Press, 1997.

Merchant, Carolyn. *The Death of Nature: Women, Ecology, and the Scientific Revolution.* New York: HarperCollins, 1989.

Moorehead, Warren K. *The Cahokia Mounds.* Edited by John E. Kell. Tuscaloosa: University of Alabama Press, 2000.

Nabokov, Peter. *Native American Testimony: A Chronicle of Indian-white Relations from Prophecy to the Present, 1492-2000.* New York: Penguin, 1991.

North Carolina Division of Parks and Recreation of the Dept of Natural and Cultural Resources. "History Highlights." *Dismal Swamp State Park.* n.d. https://www.ncparks.gov/dismal-swamp-state-park/history.

NSF Public Affairs, "Largest, oldest Maya monument suggests importance of communal work," National Science Foundation. 18 June 2020. https://www.nsf.gov/discoveries/disc_summ.jsp?cntn_id=300785.

Oatis, Steven J. *A Colonial Complex: South Carolina's Frontiers in the Era of the Yamasee War, 1680-1730*. Lincoln: University of Nebraska Press, 2004.

O'Brien, Cormac. *The Forgotten History of America: Little-Known Conflicts of Lasting Importance from the Earliest Colonists to the Eve of the Revolution*. New York: Crestline, 2008.

Prockter, J. "Map of East and West Florida, 1760." State Archives of Florida. *Florida Memory*. 1760. https://www.floridamemory.com/items/show/323257. Map.

Raab, James W. *Spain, Britain and the American Revolution in Florida, 1763-1783*. Jefferson: McFarland & Company.

Rashid, Samory. *Black Muslims in the U.S.: History, Politics, and the Struggle of a Community*. New York: Palgrave Macmillan, 2013.

Rediker, Marcus. *Villains of All Nations: Atlantic Pirates in the Golden Age*. Boston: Beacon Press, 2004.

Rivers, Larry Eugene. *Slavery in Florida: Territorial Days to Emancipation*. Tallahassee: University of Florida Press, 2008.

Rodney, Walter. *A History of the Upper Guinea Coast, 1545 to 1800*. Oxford University Press, 1970.

Rodney, Walter. *How Europe Underdeveloped Africa*. London: Bogle-L'Ouverture Publications, 1972.

Salmon, Emily Jones, and John Salmon. "Tobacco in Colonial Virginia." *Encyclopedia Virginia*. 5 February 2021. https://encyclopedia-virginia.org/entries/tobacco-in-colonial-virginia.

Shamlin, Jim. "The Tuscarora War." *North Carolina Literary Review*. Vol. 1, No. 1. Summer, 1992.

Shirley, Neal, and Saralee Stafford. *Dixie Be Damned: 500 Years of Insurrection in the American South*. Oakland: AK Press, 2015.

Siebert, Wilbur H. *Loyalists in East Florida, 1774-1784*. Vol. 1. Boston: Gregg Press, 1929.

Smallwood, Arwin. "Tri-Racial Identity of Tuscarora, Meherrin, Melungeon and Other Native Americans in North Carolina, Virginia and East to West." *The Michael Eure Show Podcast.* 17 December 2020. https://www.waketech.edu/student-services/student-advocacy/podcasts/michael-eure-show/tri-racial-identity-tuscarora-meherrin

"Spanish map of the Saint Augustine area." State Archives of Florida, *Florida Memory.* 1771. https://www.floridamemory.com/items/show/33665, Accessed 1 January 2022.

"Tolomato Indian Village," *Historical Marker Database.* n.d. https://www.hmdb.org/m.asp?m=47389.

de Vargas Machuca, Tomas Lopez. "Plano de la Ciudad y Puerto de San Agustin de la Florida." 1783. Map

Worth, John E. "Spanish Missions." *New Georgia Encyclopedia.* 8 June 2017. https://www.georgiaencyclopedia.org/articles/arts-culture/spanish-missions.

Zonneveld, Andrew, "Archeological excavation of the second Fort Mose." Photograph. 18 July 2021.

Zonneveld, Andrew, "Entrance to Fort Mose Historic State Park." Photograph. 18 July 2021.

INDEX

Y

ON OUR OWN AUTHORITY! PUBLISHING

Founded in 2012, On Our Own Authority! is a volunteer-run
autonomous research press based in Atlanta, Georgia.
We specialize in anarchist literature and global radical history,
emphasizing themes of anti-colonialism, direct democracy, and
workers' self-management.

www.oooabooks.org

OTHER TITLES NOW AVAILABLE:

Ole Birk Laursen,
*Lay Down Your Arms:
Anti-Militarism, Anti-Imperialism, and the Global Radical Left in
the 1930s*

Modibo Kadalie,
Pan-African Social Ecology

Joseph Edwards,
Workers' Self-Management in the Caribbean

Christian Høgsbjerg,
Chris Braithwaite: Mariner, Renegade and Castaway

Sen Katayama,
The Labor Movement in Japan

Kimathi Mohammed,
Organization and Spontaneity

Faith Beauchemin,
How Queer!
Personal narratives from bisexual, pansexual, polysexual, sexually-
fluid, and other non-monosexual perspectives

Ida B. Wells,
Lynch Law in Georgia & Other Writings

Eusi Kwayana,
The Bauxite Strike and the Old Politics

Nani Ferreira-Mathews,
Birthright?
Travelogue of and American Radical in Israel/Palestine

David Weir,
Jean Vigo and the Anarchist Eye

Lenni Brenner,
Zionism in the Age of the Dictators

Emma Goldman and Alexander Berkman,
To Remain Silent is Impossible

Andrew Zonneveld, editor,
The Commune: Paris, 1871